D0835533

# Marketing

To Lynn, Karen, Nicola and Sarah,
the best 'test-marketeers' in the business,
and to Hilary for all her typing.

# Marketing

Arnold Fewell and Neville Wills

*Series Editor:* John O'Connor

Butterworth-Heinemann Ltd
Linacre House, Jordan Hill, Oxford OX2 8DP

PART OF REED INTERNATIONAL BOOKS

OXFORD   LONDON   BOSTON
MUNICH   NEW DELHI   SINGAPORE   SYDNEY
TOKYO   TORONTO   WELLINGTON

First published 1992
Reprinted 1993

**British Library Cataloguing in Publication Data**
Fewell, Arnold
   Marketing. – (Hospitality Managers'
   Pocket Book Series)
   I. Title II. Wills, Neville III. Series
   642.068

ISBN 0 7506 0165 5

Composition by Genesis Typesetting, Rochester, Kent
Printed in England by Clays Ltd, St Ives plc

# Contents

# Preface

This book has one very clear objective. It is to get rid of the mystique that surrounds the word 'marketing'. Therefore the language is simple and marketing jargon is avoided. Where it is used it is fully explained. Five case studies are developed throughout the book to show how different managers within the hospitality industry might approach a particular marketing situation. These case studies relate to a hotel, a public house, a restaurant, a fast-food restaurant and a staff restaurant.

Initially this book looks at ways of analysing where your business is today and reviews how your services may need to be developed to meet customer expectations. It shows how a strategic framework can be developed with other chapters on the use of the tactical tools: advertising, sales promotion, pubic relations, personal selling, merchandising and direct mail.

Each chapter is summarized and finishes with a number of key questions that you can consider and relate to your own business and management responsibilities. However, the practical approach and style of the book will also provide students with a valuable insight into how classroom theory can be effectively used within the industry.

It is the book that we wish we had been able to read both at college and during our years in hotel and catering management. It would have become a constant reference point. We could have reduced risk when we wanted to try something new and ensured that we monitored the various promotional activities effectively to maximize profit. This would have saved us considerable sums of money.

There is a saying that 'I never make the same mistake twice, I make new ones every day'. This experience has been built into the book to provide you with practical advice when and where appropriate. This will help you save money, reduce wasted effort and lessen the pain of making mistakes.

As this book goes to print we are in a period of economic hardship where many people are struggling to stay in business. Marketing activity is being cut back at the very time it is most needed. However, those businesses that learn more about effective marketing will reap the benefits of staying in business, sustaining profitability and be better equipped to take advantage of economic growth when it comes.

*Arnold Fewell*
*Neville Wills*

# 1
# What is marketing?

## Introduction

'Marketing is simple, it has to be otherwise I wouldn't understand it.' These words started the first marketing presentation I ever attended. My immediate reaction was to dismiss the statement, especially when I remembered my days at college. However, the more I read, the more I practised the principles, the more I realized it was true.

This book sets out to make marketing simple, so that you can use the principles to improve the profitability of your business. It tries to avoid marketing jargon, but if this is used it is fully explained. It will help all managers, at all levels, within the hospitality industry: from hoteliers to publicans, restaurateurs to contract caterers, guest house owners to public sector caterers.

## So, what is marketing?

The Chartered Institute of Marketing defines it as 'The management process responsible for identifying, anticipating and satisfying customer requirements profitably.'

This definition splits into four parts:

1 The marketing oriented manager ensures that all parts of the business share the same philosophy, from the receptionist to the kitchen porter. It is a team effort, with complete involvement to achieve the key objectives.

2  The continued satisfaction of the customer is the purpose of your business. You need to identify what they require now and, based on all available information, anticipate what they will require in the future. The customer is king and as such should be revered.

3  Profit keeps you in business. However, you need sustained profit. That is profit that can be built upon year on year and the most valuable contributor to a solid business base is repeat business; the customer keeps coming back for more.

4  No successful business is static. It changes and develops according to a variety of factors. It is vital that your business is constantly reviewed so that it can react to changes in the marketplace. This process needs to be managed and planned in a logical manner.

## The marketing process: a cyclical activity

This process needs to be applied with discipline. Marketing is ongoing, it is repetitive and thus has been described as a cyclical activity. This is not entirely accurate because, by describing it as cyclical or circular, it suggests that you start again at exactly the same point. Those who go round and round in circles often chase things they can never achieve.

You need to look at it more as a bicycle wheel. After each revolution the bicycle has moved closer to its destination. Similarly, the marketing process moves on after each revolution and takes the business closer to its long-term objectives.

There are various stages of the marketing cycle, which are identified in Figure 1.1.

The process starts by undertaking research into the requirements of the customer and the market.

It continues by changing the service or product to match the needs of the customer based on the research findings.

The new and improved service needs to be promoted to both existing and potential clients.

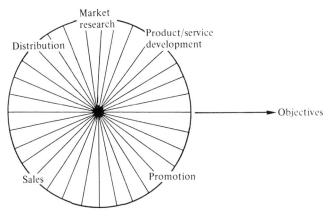

**Figure 1.1** The marketing cycle

Promotion generates awareness and interest which lead to enquiries. Now salesmanship plays a part, not pushy but genuinely interested in meeting the specific needs of the customer as an individual.

Once sold, the customer must have the promised service delivered and here again so much will depend on your people, the staff, providing the right levels of service to ensure customer satisfaction. Distribution involves all your staff, from the first point of enquiry to the payment of the bill. But, even in a service industry, distribution is not just about people, it is also about the physical layout of the establishment so that service may be efficient and the customer may feel at ease and comfortable.

At the end of the first cycle you will need to review how successful your marketing strategy has been:

- By researching customer reaction and take-up.
- By modifying products or services further.
- By more effective promotion.
- By better selling.
- By better distribution.

and so on, as you progress towards clearly expressed objectives. The whole operation, whether it be a hotel, restaurant, public house, wine bar or canteen, should become more effective in meeting your customers' needs, matching expectations in terms of service and value for money.

## The aims of this book

This book is designed to help you:

1 Understand the various parts of the marketing cycle and how they interact.
2 Run a diagnostic check on your business.
3 Produce a plan to improve profit performance and service levels.
4 Maximize your profitability through more effective communication with both your customers and staff.

These objectives apply across the board to all aspects of the hospitality industry but, as a further resource, we shall be considering the situations of five establishments to see how the application of marketing may be used to address weaknesses and develop opportunities.

### *The hotel*

This two-star, 40-bedroom hotel, with 30 private bathrooms, is situated in a medium-sized market town. It currently obtains 35 per cent of its accommodation business mid-week and 65 per cent at week-ends. It has three good-sized function rooms. These can cope with meetings for 10 to 200 people and with weddings and dinner dances for up to 150. It is owned by a family living in Jersey but has had a chequered history, with three managers employed in the last four years. The current manager has just been appointed and comes from a major hotel chain. He has one assistant manager, a head chef, a housekeeper and a restaurant supervisor making up his management team. The standards are inconsistent due to the high turnover of management and staff and this has resulted in a poor local reputation. The hotel is in need of redecoration both inside and out. It is easily seen as travellers approach by car. However, it is on the corner of a pedestrian-only area and there are no signs to the car park, thus most people continue on their journey because access is unclear. The hotel has always made a profit but, over the last three years, that profit has been declining by an average of 15 per cent per annum. It is forecast that this year the hotel will lose £25,000.

## The restaurant

This has recently been refurbished throughout. It was originally farm outbuildings but first became a pub before being extended 10 years ago into a restaurant. It is part of a small chain of restaurants. It is situated two miles outside a major conference town. However, its mainstay business is passing travellers and local families from within a seven-mile radius. It looks after children well, with a children's play area and a special all-inclusive menu at £1.50. The adult menu is centred on steaks and traditional English food and has an average spend of £10.25 on food and £2.75 on liquor. It has 75 covers and a very good Saturday night and Sunday lunch restaurant business when it turns over the tables at least twice. Its main weekday business is local bar trade and bar snacks. The wine list is a basic selection of 15 wines, ranging from £5.50 to £10.75.

## The pub

The landlord is new to the business and has no catering qualification other than attending a brewery course. He tries to provide a very wide range of products and services and be all things to all people. He offers a regular selection of evening entertainment from quizzes to country and western music. There are several pub teams competing in the local competitions. A major office block is under a mile away but less than 10 per cent of the lunchtime business comes from this source.

The pub provides a range of reasonably priced bar lunches Tuesday to Sunday. It is run by the publican, his wife and her parents. There is a very heavy customer bias towards the older age groups, i.e. 50 plus, however they are all regular users. It is situated on the outskirts of a small town with good car parking. The landlord has high borrowings and is struggling to make sufficient profit to cover them.

## The staff restaurant

It can only just be described as a staff restaurant because many of the old canteen images remain. The catering manager is close to retirement but the new assistant is very keen to make changes. The place looks tired and the menu is unimaginative. Some attempts have been made to hold special food events but these are spasmodic. They are badly advertised and thus poorly attended. The food is hot and the daily specials are well cooked and wholesome but poorly presented. The staff have been there for approximately five years and have run out of steam. However, the assistant has bought new service equipment to improve the situation but is fighting to gain acceptance of her ideas. The number of customers using the restaurant in the last two years has fallen from 250 to less than 100, with the average spend remaining constant at 85p.

## The fast-food restaurant

This is situated in the high street of a busy market town. It is open from 10 a.m. to 10 p.m., seven days a week and has 60 covers and a busy take-away operation. The menu is based on a variety of burgers, chips and a selection of drinks. It is owned by a local businessman but run by an experienced manager and his well-trained staff. There is no fast-food competition in the town at present but this is not expected to continue for long. The premises were upgraded 18 months ago and the décor and fittings are clean, relaxing and comfortable. It has a good local reputation built on service and value for money, and has become a popular meeting place during the day.

To provide further assistance at the end of each chapter there will be a summary of the main points, along with some key questions to ask yourself about your business.

## Summary

1 Marketing is a simple process that is concerned with identifying and satisfying customer needs at a profit.
2 The process is ongoing and requires constant attention to ensure you match customer expectations in terms of service and value for money.

## Key questions

1 How would you describe your business?
2 How important is marketing, within your current business operation, in achieving increased profitability?
3 How could marketing help these five very different businesses?

# 2
# Customer-oriented management

## From the guest's point of view

A catering student working behind the bar was discussing with a hotel resident what he had done at college that day. Apparently he had been involved in a discussion about who should write a hotel brochure, the choice being between the hotel manager and the hotel customer. Sadly, no outright decision had been reached.

The ideal situation would be for the brochure to be written by a customer, not any old customer but, specifically, a business resident to write the hotel brochure aimed at the business customer, or a Sunday lunch customer to sing the praises of the way in which the restaurant caters for all the family.

However:

1  Customers do not write brochures, at least not normally. Peel potatoes, yes, though cash is the preferable way to have accounts settled. Nevertheless, unsolicited testimonials from highly satisfied customers do no harm at all.
2  You need to put yourself in the customers' shoes to perceive not only what they require but the statements and claims which will make them understand that you mean business, their business.

3  You will have a range of different products and services and you have a spectrum of different customers, e.g. the hotel resident could be staying for a variety of reasons – business, week-end break, attending a function, a training course or a conference. Each type of customer will be looking for different facilities in the hotel.

The skill that must be cultivated is the matching of the needs of the customers with the right mix and level of services. You cannot write a paragraph about the hotel bedrooms and expect it to appeal to all your different types of resident. You cannot expect notes on leisure activities to appeal to all groups, and mention of conference facilities may well be a right turn-off for the person trying to get away from it all.

In other words, you must become customer oriented. This is not as easy as it sounds because you normally look at your business from an operational point of view, whereas what matters is how your customer perceives you. In other words it is not so much horses for courses as courses for horses, speaking of which, one technique is to use the blinkers.

Horses wear them to narrow their span of vision so that they concentrate on winning the race. You can pretend to wear blinkers as you tour your business and just concentrate on one particular operational aspect. This could be signage.

Concentrate solely on looking at all signs to ensure that they direct customers clearly and easily to the various parts of the establishment.

Ask yourself these questions:

- Can customers in the bar find their way to the toilets?
- Is the restaurant easy to find in the high-rise office block?
- How do hotel residents find their way back to reception from their bedrooms?

Always place yourself in the customer's position. After a short period of practice this will become second nature.

## You don't get a second chance to make a first impression

This statement was first given to me as advice on preparing for a job interview. It shows the importance of those first few seconds as you walk through the door to shake hands with a prospective employer. However, it is just as important for the customer-oriented manager.

Customers will often base their impression of your business on their first contact. This is unlikely to be as they walk through your front door. In a hotel, restaurant or public house it could be a telephone call to make an enquiry about a room, a dinner reservation or a function.

You need to examine how that first contact is handled:

- Did the phone ring for a minute or was it answered by the end of the third ring?
- Was the customer kept waiting while the right person was found, or were they put through immediately to the right person?
- How was the enquiry converted into a booking? If it wasn't, what action is planned to achieve this?

When the customer's first impression is good it makes it easier to continue that experience. Too often the first impression is poor, and then too much time is spent on trying to rescue the situation.

The first impression can be encountered in a variety of ways, such as a menu display, a letter, an advertisement, a brochure, a receptionist or a directional sign.

## I know what my customer wants

When I joined North Yorkshire County Council as Catering Manager I was told that all the children wanted was chips. If these weren't available each day then the customers would stop using the facility. This was usually added to the fact that, because Macdonalds was successful with the young, they also only wanted burgers. The result was that all the cash cafeteria menus were built around burgers and chips. This resulted in fewer and fewer children using the service because it was not what they wanted every day.

When market research was carried out a very different picture emerged. The children wanted healthier eating, better presentation, greater variety, less queuing, consistent portions, good value for money, good quality ingredients and pleasant surroundings to eat in. I have always argued that this is a pretty good list for every catering operation to aim at. However, until this point schoolchildren had not been viewed as customers, who came to school with £1 in their pockets and the ability to spend it in either the school restaurant or the shop round the corner.

If it had been true that all the children wanted was chips, and these were always available, then it should follow that the customers were happy. The numbers having a meal would be high and constant. Nothing could have been further from the truth. The customers were voting with their feet. The situation became so serious that only 21 per cent of the pupils were using the service. When the results of the research were implemented the numbers rose dramatically. Within three years 56 per cent of the pupils were staying for a school lunch.

We will look at market research in greater detail in Chapter 4.

All levels of management and staff can, and must, talk to customers to find out their attitudes to your business. To do this successfully they must ask appropriate questions.

## Establishing rapport: open and closed questions

In my hotel days there used to be a daily event called 'the assistant manager's dash'. The idea was to start at one end of the restaurant and ask each diner 'Are you enjoying the meal?' This nearly always received the answer 'Yes' and enabled the assistant manager to move quickly to the next table.

The object was to see how quickly every diner could be spoken to, so that the next morning the hotel manager could be told that there were no complaints and everybody had enjoyed their meal.

Unless one makes a conscious effort, it is much easier to ask a closed question, that is one that can simply be answered with a 'yes' or 'no'. It means that little information is gathered, no conversation is developed and therefore no rapport is established with customers. No rapport means a lack of confidence in your service, which will make a sale more difficult to achieve.

When an open question is used, that is, one beginning with 'how', 'what', 'why', 'where', 'when' or 'who', then the reverse is achieved. So, 'How are you enjoying your meal?' is going to draw out both good and bad comments from the customers. It will also provide the chance to probe further, that is, to ask another question as a result of the first question. This process will lead to a two-way conversation, will put customers at ease and will show that you are genuinely interested in their comments.

The same technique can be used in a sales situation. It enables you to find out more about potential customers and what they may be looking for from hotel, restaurant, conference or catering facilities. The more you ask open questions the more you will find out, and the easier it will be to match what a customer is looking for with what you have to offer.

## Standards matter

Customers have certain standards that they expect. These standards will vary according to individual customers' perceptions. The standards of a four-star hotel will vary from those of a two-star. This will be in the type and style of the facilities available, the standard of décor, the level of staffing and the price charged. Both ratings can offer value for money and will appeal to different types of customer. It is a question of matching levels of service with customers' perceptions.

The important fact is that a standard has been set by the manager. Standards are minimum levels of service that must not be reduced. They must be consistent so that customers receive the same treatment from one visit to another. The key to achieving set standards is for you, the manager, to set an example and, when and where necessary, to reinforce standards through training. (See Chapter 16.)

Training must be customer-oriented and match the style and image of your establishment. You will need to create a check-list for all areas of the business. From this you can identify both standards and training needs.

So if you are showing a new bar person how to set up the bar snack display, it must be done from the customer's side. This will ensure that attention is given to the way it looks, the placement of self-service cutlery with handles pointing towards the customer, the labelling of each dish, all aimed at making the customer's choice easier and more enjoyable. Customers do not compromise, so don't compromise your business.

Of course there are a whole range of management problems and decisions that have to be made. They may relate to finance, staffing, the fabric of the building, the product or the customers. Different managers will have their own priorities, maybe their own favourites. The accounts-oriented manager will put financial matters at the top of the list. A personnel-oriented manager will change this and put staffing as a number one.

Marketing-oriented managers always put the customer first. In fact, they go one stage further by trying to think like a typical customer of the business they are working in.

## Summary

1 Everyone in the hospitality industry needs to become customer oriented.
2 The customer's complete satisfaction is the purpose of your business.

3 The first impression you give to a customer is vital, it is likely to have occurred well before they walk through the front door.

4 Never believe that you know what customers want without asking them.

5 Open questions should be used to establish customer attitudes.

6 Set minimum standards for all parts of your business and provide the appropriate training for staff.

## Key questions

1 How customer oriented are you?
2 What is the first impression you give to your customers?
3 What have customers told you about your business?
4 What minimum standards have you set, and do they cover all parts of your operation?

# 3
# Where is your business?

Well-constructed marketing strategies and plans are dependent on a clear-sighted, objective diagnosis of the current situation, a business health-check. Which customers use which services the most, how much and how often, and just how well are you doing compared to the competition? How well are you maintaining the right levels of service? Is your trade growing or declining? Are you overlooking opportunities, or what should you be doing to exploit them?

This chapter provides a framework to help you run a diagnostic check over your business so that you can decide not only what needs to be done but what changes and improvements may have to be implemented if you are to achieve new objectives.

## The business health-check

A great deal has been said and written about preventive medicine. This is where considerable resources have been put into promoting a healthier lifestyle with better diets, more regular exercise, no smoking and reduction of alcohol intake. The purpose is to take more care of the body so that it continues to function effectively. There are a number of diagnostic checks that a doctor might use to ensure that this is so. These might include height-to-weight ratio, pulse, blood pressure and urine samples.

The business health-check is similar. It looks at three key areas of the business to find out what shape and level of fitness the business is in. Perhaps it is overweight, with too many staff for the level of business, or the pulse is weak with insufficient sales coming in. The three areas for closer examination are:

1 product,
2 customers,
3 competition.

## What are the benefits?

You will see more clearly:

1 Your strengths and weaknesses.
2 Threats and opportunities, in terms of changes in customer needs or competitor activity.
3 Which services should be enhanced, which should be dropped.
4 Where to use scarce resources – staffing, promotional spend, service improvements – to grow your business more effectively.

## The product

You will need to identify all your product offerings. For example, a hotelier may offer accommodation to: mid-week business users/weekend leisure breaks/conferences/training courses/guests attending a wedding or dinner-dance, etc. Then, of course, there will be all the food and beverage products, the different function markets: the list will vary from one hotel to another.

Each of these products make up the total turnover and profit contribution of your business. However, this contribution will not be equally spread; maybe leisure accommodation contributes more than business trade, or function trade more than restaurant sales. Turnover and profit contribution of each product need to be identified separately.

For example, in the public house case study, the bar snack operation was open Tuesday to Sunday 12 till 2 p.m. and 7 to 9.30 p.m. However, lunchtime accounted for 80 per cent of the food profit against the evenings, when most of the 20 per cent was taken towards the end of the week and at the weekend. Tuesday and Wednesday struggled to run at breakeven, i.e. where sales matched the cost of food, staff and overheads. The landlord closed on Mondays to give all the catering staff the day off and ease pressure on the rota. This analysis of the profit contribution suggested that he might do better to open Monday lunchtime to attract new and existing customers and not serve bar snacks on Monday, Tuesday and Wednesday evenings.

## The customer

Customers come in all shapes and sizes, so how can we analyse them?

1 By user type. Which of the products you have identified do they use? Is it just business accommodation, or is it business accommodation and the company's annual dinner and dance? Is the same customer a business user mid-week and a leisure user at the weekends? You need to answer these questions for each type of customer.
2 By frequency. How often do customers buy? Does the customer buy daily, weekly, monthly or annually? Is the purchase for just one product or for several? This will establish where you can obtain new business from existing customers as well as identify customers who have stopped using you.
3 By value. Each customer group has a different spending intention. But how much is this, and is the average spend per head changing? If it was in decline it might indicate that demand was lower or the standards of your service were slipping. Until you identify *what* is happening, you cannot decide what you need to investigate more thoroughly.
4 By time of purchase. When does the customer decide to

purchase? Is it last-minute chance business, or do they book up to several months in advance? This information will be vital when you plan your sales activity because you would match the buying pattern with the timing of your personal sales call.

5 By attitude. Which customers always use you as the first choice and which use you only as a last resort? What do they really think about your business, including both good and bad points?

| Services: \ Customers: | Business persons – local | Business persons – travellers | Businesses – local | Businesses – out of town | Local/professional organizations | Local residents – families | Local residents – individuals | Tourists | Clubs |
|---|---|---|---|---|---|---|---|---|---|
| Accommodation - business | | X | X | X | X | | | | |
| Accommodation - leisure | | | | | | X | X | X | |
| Conferences | X | X | X | X | X | | | | X |
| Training courses | X | X | X | X | X | | | | X |
| Lunches - business | | | X | | X | | | | X |
| Business dinners | | | X | X | X | | | | |
| Dinner dances | | | X | | X | | | | X |
| Bar snacks | X | X | X | X | | X | X | X | |
| Bar liquor sales | X | X | X | X | X | X | X | X | X |
| Weddings | | | | | X | | | | |
| Leisure lunches | | | | | | X | X | X | |
| Leisure dinners | | | | | | X | X | X | |
| Day meetings | | X | X | X | X | | | | X |
| Staff lunches | | | X | | | | | | |
| Staff dinners | | | X | | | | | | |
| Institutional meals | | | | | X | | | | X |
| | | | | | | | | | |
| | | | | | | | | | |
| | | | | | | | | | |
| | | | | | | | | | |

**Figure 3.1** The service/customer matrix

The service/customer matrix helps you to identify which types of customer use which of your services. The same customer group may well buy not one service but several, i.e. the business customer may buy lunches, or accommodation, or conference and training facilities. Unless you have established who buys what you do not know where your business lies. Figure 3.1 shows a completed matrix for our hotel case study.

## The competition

It is not just a question of identifying the competitors and writing down every hotel, restaurant and public house in the area. You need to refer back to each of your products and identify precisely those competitors who really are a possible threat either now or into the future. This analysis would look at the competition by:

1 Type. Is the competition to your bar snack operation the public house opposite, a café in the high street, the staff restaurant at the nearby factory, another hotel or local restaurant?
2 Location. Are they in a more or less favourable part of the town, or does more or less potential custom pass their door?
3 Access. Is it easier to get to the competitor and if you need to go by car how easy is it to park? Access can change with the unwelcome arrival of roadworks or a new one-way system. The effects on both you and your competitor could be considerable over a long period of time.
4 Popularity. Who are the market leaders for any customer groups or types of service? It may be one business or several.
5 Innovation. Which competitor is most active in developing its business either by product development or by promotion?

Now, to put the competition into perspective, you need to complete two more matrices: competition and service or product offering, and competition and customer groups (see Figures 3.2 and 3.3). You should attempt to include your own establishment with the competition to see how you rate.

Again, we follow the hotel case study to demonstrate how this technique may be used.

| Competition: \ Customers: | Short stay leisure | Long stay leisure | One-night business | Two or more nights business | Conference delegates | Training course delegates | Local business | Passers-by | Local clubs | Local organizations | Local residents | | | |
|---|---|---|---|---|---|---|---|---|---|---|---|---|---|---|
| Mary's Café | | | | | | | X | X | | | X | | | |
| The King's Head Steakbar | | | | | | | X | X | X | X | X | | | |
| The Peppermill Restaurant | | | | | | | X | X | X | X | X | | | |
| The Yorkshire Arms (pub) | | | | | X | | X | X | X | X | X | | | |
| The Durham Ox (pub) | X | | X | | X | X | X | X | X | X | X | | | |
| The Hot Potato Bar | | | | | | | X | X | | | X | | | |
| The Curry House | | | | | | | X | X | X | X | X | | | |
| The Chinese Garden | | | | | | | X | X | X | X | X | | | |
| The White House Hotel | X | X | X | X | X | X | X | X | X | X | X | | | |
| The Golden Fleece | X | X | X | X | | | X | X | X | X | X | | | |
| The Italian Pizzeria | | | | | | | X | X | | | X | | | |
| | | | | | | | | | | | | | | |
| | | | | | | | | | | | | | | |
| | | | | | | | | | | | | | | |
| | | | | | | | | | | | | | | |
| | | | | | | | | | | | | | | |
| | | | | | | | | | | | | | | |
| | | | | | | | | | | | | | | |
| | | | | | | | | | | | | | | |
| | | | | | | | | | | | | | | |

**Figure 3.2** The customer/competition matrix

| Competition: \ Services: | Accommodation only | All inclusive package accommodation | Conference facilities | Training courses | Day meetings | Private lunches | Private dinners | Dinner dances | Weddings | Restaurant lunch | Restaurant dinner | Bar liquor facilities | Bar snack lunches | Bar snack dinners | Morning coffee and afternoon tea |
|---|---|---|---|---|---|---|---|---|---|---|---|---|---|---|---|
| Mary's Café | | | | | | | | | | X | | | X | | X |
| The King's Head steakbar | | | | | | X | X | X | X | X | X | X | X | | |
| The Peppermill Restaurant | | | | | | X | X | | X | X | X | | | | X |
| The Yorkshire Arms (pub) | | | | | X | X | X | X | X | X | X | X | X | | |
| The Durham Ox (pub) | X | | | | X | X | X | | | X | X | X | X | X | X |
| The Hot Potato Bar | | | | | | | | | | | | | X | | X |
| The Curry House | | | | | | | | | | X | X | | | | |
| The Chinese Garden | | | | | | | | | | X | X | | | | |
| The White House Hotel | X | X | X | X | X | X | X | X | X | X | X | X | X | X | X |
| The Golden Fleece | X | X | | | | X | X | | X | X | X | X | X | X | |
| The Italian Pizzeria | | | | | | | | | | X | X | X | X | X | |
| | | | | | | | | | | | | | | | |
| | | | | | | | | | | | | | | | |
| | | | | | | | | | | | | | | | |
| | | | | | | | | | | | | | | | |
| | | | | | | | | | | | | | | | |
| | | | | | | | | | | | | | | | |
| | | | | | | | | | | | | | | | |
| | | | | | | | | | | | | | | | |
| | | | | | | | | | | | | | | | |

**Figure 3.3** The competition/service matrix

You now begin the business health-check. You know where your business is and how it may compare with the competition in terms of market share. Next you need to identify what you may need to do to improve your performance. To start the process you need to carry out a SWOT analysis.

## SWOT analysis

Too often when a business analysis is unstructured, the results are confused and subjective. SWOT analysis overcomes this by concentrating your thoughts on four key areas of assessment.

SWOT is an acronym for Strengths, Weaknesses, Opportunities and Threats. It provides a framework for assessment of the information you have gathered about your business.

Strengths may include: a good local reputation, prime site location, low staff turnover or dominance of key markets, e.g. first choice for wedding receptions. Once identified, strengths can be built on.

Weaknesses can range from old premises which require upgrading to lack of social skills among the staff. You ignore weaknesses at your peril; the purpose of identifying them is so that you may plan to reduce or eliminate them.

Weaknesses and strengths are matters of customer perception. It is not what you think that counts – in the next chapter we look at research methods which will help you to find out what other people think, objectively.

The third element is business opportunities. How can current weaknesses be developed into new strengths? Equally, present strengths may be enhanced to overcome threats.

Threats may also be internal and external factors. They may threaten the profitable future of the business. It could be the possibility of a major competitor moving into your area, or a new by-pass which will take chance trade away, or the pending retirement of your head chef after 20 years.

In the planning process you will be looking at ways to minimize the effect of these threats.

SWOT analysis takes time and effort. Practical experience shows that it is a worthwhile investment. It is not just a question of analysing statistics, it requires creative interpretation and lateral thought.

Below we have identified a possible SWOT analysis for our fast food restaurant situated in a busy market town.

## *Strengths*

Good high street location.
Very popular at lunchtimes.
Experienced manager who is well known in the area.
Staff are efficient and welcoming.
Décor is relaxing and comfortable.
Prices are good value for money.
No fast-food competition.
Good reputation.

## *Weaknesses*

Receive complaints about the amount of litter that accumulates outside the premises.
Town is quiet after 6 p.m. and business is very slack.
Kitchen equipment is not fast enough to cope with peak demand.
Local authority will not allow new illuminated shop signage.
It is becoming increasingly difficult to recruit staff as unemployment in the area is low and the number of children leaving school is in decline.
Menu is limited.
Concern by local environmental group about the excessive use of packaging.

## *Opportunities*

To provide a home delivery service after 6 p.m. using motorbikes with hot cabinets.
To attract women returners to work by offering job share, flexible working and part-time work. Hold an open evening to show the type and style of the work involved.
Place new large litter bins outside the premises. Sponsor three litter bins in the area with the local authority. This will reduce litter.

Introduce re-cycled disposables.

Arrange an aluminium can collection system, with money raised going to local children's hospital.

Reduce peak pressure at lunchtime by providing a price discount between 2.15 p.m. and 2.45 p.m., also to attract late lunchtime customers.

Review new menu items to extend the variety.

## Threats

New fast-food outlet planned by national chain.

Possibility of manager being 'poached' to open this new operation.

Changes in government legislation about litter and the responsibility for its collection.

New factory opening on the outskirts of town which will further reduce the labour market.

Growing activity of healthy eating lobby in the area.

A SWOT analysis will generate a list of information needs. There will be areas of assumption that have been made that will require further research; they must be clarified and confirmed otherwise your decision-making process will be flawed from the outset. If we look at the fast-food restaurant example we might decide to establish:

1 That the customers' perception of the staff is welcoming and efficient.
2 That the customers find the décor relaxing and comfortable.
3 That the prices do represent good value.
4 How many customers are in town after 6 p.m.
5 Customers' perception of the limited menu choice.

This information is needed before we can ascertain if it is the right decision to introduce a new menu or expand into home delivery after 6 p.m.

Opportunities create an element of risk. Whenever risk is involved, we need to assess its possible impact. We also need

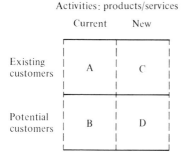

Figure 3.4 Activities/services framework

to assess which opportunities are realistic. To do this the following framework is useful:

Look at Figure 3.4 and consider:

● *Which existing activities/services need to be developed or limited.*
● *Which new services need to be developed.*

*A* is the sector of least risks. You are selling existing products into your existing customers. But you have three options:

1  Carry on as you are.
2  Seek to develop your sales further.
3  Decide to withdraw from this, your traditional business, in favour of a more profitable initiative.

Even in this position you need to know about your current market and potential markets before you can safely decide what course to take.

*B* is a new market into which you wish to sell your existing products. It is likely that the knowledge you have gained of your existing market will help, but you would be wrong to assume that the new market has exactly the same characteristics.

*C* is the sector in which you are introducing new products into your existing market. You will need to test the product thoroughly to ensure that it will be acceptable and that its introduction will not put your traditional business at risk.

*D* is the area of greatest risk with a new product in a new market. This will require detailed research into the marketplace.

In this chapter we have looked at types of information that are available within the business and from its customers. To make the best decision in the future we need to base these decisions on the widest range of information. This requires further market research, the subject of the next chapter.

## Summary

1  You need to gain a complete picture of where your business is at.
2  The business health-check concentrates on the key areas of product, customers and the competition.
3  SWOT analysis helps identify the strengths, weaknesses, opportunities and threats of the business.
4  Opportunities have various elements of risk, and these must be identified.

## Key questions

1  What information do you have readily available, and what other information do you need?
2  What does your SWOT analysis tell you?
3  How much risk do you want to take, or can afford to take?
4  How do you want to re-position your business within the marketplace?

# 4
# Market research

## You can never know too much about customers

In the business health-check we looked at a customer analysis which covered areas such as user type and frequency. However there are other ways in which customers can be analysed. This will be very important when we start to look at the promotional mix in Chapters 8 to 12. The first system looks at customers' age, sex, location, behaviour and demographic groupings produced by the Joint Industry Council on Newspaper Advertising Research. This breaks down the community into six groups or social classes. It is based on what people do for a living and therefore on the amount of disposable income they have. The groups are described in Table 4.1.

The distribution of these groups all vary considerably across the county. In some areas the classification will change. Pensioners are often living on the subsistence line. However, in some areas they will have bought a retirement home, having moved from an expensive housing area such as the south east. They will have savings, no family commitments, no mortgage repayments and will thus have a considerable disposable income.

The second system of customer analysis comes under the name of ACORN. This classifies consumers by type of residential area in which they live. ACORN stands for *A Classification Of Residential Neighbourhoods*. It links people's addresses to their likely lifestyle and hence to their potential purchasing habits. The eleven groups are described in Table 4.2.

**Table 4.1**

| Group classification | Class | Status |
|---|---|---|
| A | Upper middle | Higher managerial and administrative staff |
| B | Middle | Intermediate professional management and administrative staff |
| C1 | Lower middle | Supervisory, clerical and junior management positions |
| C2 | Skilled working | Skilled manual workers |
| D | Working | Semi and unskilled manual workers |
| E | At the lowest level of subsistence | Casual and lowest grade workers, pensioners and widows. |

**Table 4.2**

| | |
|---|---|
| Group A | Agricultural areas |
| Group B | Modern family housing – high incomes |
| Group C | Older housing of intermediate status |
| Group D | Poor quality terraced housing |
| Group E | Better-off council estates |
| Group F | Less well-off council estates |
| Group G | Poorest council estates |
| Group H | Multi-racial areas |
| Group I | High status, non-family areas |
| Group J | Affluent suburban housing |
| Group K | Better-off retirement areas |

This information is computer based using the publicly available census statistics. It is available from the CACI Market Analysis Group. The above groups are further split so that, in total, 39 separate types of housing or dwelling are identified.

This may be useful information for a restaurant to obtain so that it can identify the houses in its location which are more likely to afford the pleasure of eating out on a regular basis.

## Why market research?

Market research is needed to establish the base of the marketing activity. There are two basic types of research – quantative and qualitative. Quantative research requires the answers to be expressed in numerical terms. For example 23 per cent of those surveyed eat out at least once a month, or six out of every 10 diners have a starter and main course only. They are usually carried out by asking a number of people who make up a representative sample of the population. Qualitative research usually involves fewer people being interviewed but in far greater depth. This enables identification of people's attitudes and perceptions towards different products and services.

Market research can often require the use of a specialist agency. However, what we have tried to do is establish a number of areas of research that you can carry out yourself.

There are seven areas of research you could use. They are:

1 nominal group research,
2 questionnaires,
3 research interviews,
4 telephone research,
5 mail-outs,
6 desk research,
7 observation.

Different parts of the hospitality industry can use these in their own way, so we have identified different uses which illustrate their applications.

## 1 Nominal group research

This is where groups of existing and potential customers are brought together in groups of up to 20. They are put at ease by the researcher and the objective explained. A hotelier could have invited 20 local secretaries to find out how the hotel can provide a better service for the secretaries' bosses. A catering manager might have arranged for 20 office workers, selected at random, to find out their reaction to the recent series of 'special days' that have been carried out.

I believe that if you provide a benefit in this situation, then you will get far greater involvement and participation, which will assist you. In the above instances benefits could include making the secretaries' lives easier with a better hotel response to their need, or a free lunch on the next 'special day' to be held for the office workers.

Once the introduction has been completed, the mechanics are explained. The first stage is for each person to write down their own thoughts on the subject being discussed. A secretary might comment that it takes a long time for the telephone to be answered, a worker might write down that he did not know anything special was taking place – the point being that it is their individual thoughts and ideas that are being discussed.

The next stage is for the researcher to identify all the points from the group and to write each one up on a flip-chart. It is helpful if someone else is assisting to write down the various statements. It needs to be a statement that can be agreed or disagreed with, if it has the words 'should be' then this will be the case, e.g. 'the telephone should be answered more quickly'; 'the publicity for special days should be better'. Each point should be numbered. The number of people taking part in the research and the number of comments being made will determine the length of time required. It will take approximately 40 minutes to obtain 30 comments from 20 people.

The researcher needs to clarify each of the points by asking probing questions. Sometimes a person will make a statement that has a number of possible interpretations, e.g. 'the food was cold'.

This could be because the equipment was defective, the food was not hot enough when it went out, the service was slow, there were insufficient counters to take the money or the customer could not find a table. The final statement after the first point has been probed may then state 'the food should be hotter at the start of service'.

When all the points have been covered, the next stage is for the individuals to fill in a form, as seen in Table 4.3

**Table 4.3**

| Number of statement | Strongly agree | Slightly agree | Slightly disagree | Strongly disagree |
|---------------------|----------------|----------------|-------------------|-------------------|
| 1                   |                |                |                   |                   |
| 2                   |                |                |                   |                   |
| 3                   |                |                |                   |                   |
| 4                   |                |                |                   |                   |
| etc.                |                |                |                   |                   |

Each person considers the statement on the flip-chart and decides if they agree or disagree with it. There is then a further choice of 'slightly' or 'strongly' on each option. The researcher needs to explain that each person should tick the box that most matches their attitude to each of the statements. When they have ticked one box for each statement then the forms are collected.

If you wanted to analyse the results according to age and sex then you would need this information to be written on the top of each form.

At the end of the exercise you will be able to group the statements together as they will fit into loose categories. These could be food presentation, food quality, menus, ambience, attitude of staff, and many more. Each statement can be given a weighting according to how many of the group ticked each of the boxes. Thus under food preparation the described picture in Table 4.4 could emerge.

Table 4.4

| Statement | Strongly agree | Slightly agree | Slightly disagree | Strongly disagree |
|---|---|---|---|---|
| 1 The food should be better garnished | 1 | 3 | 6 | 12 |
| 2 Food service equipment should be up-dated with better lighting and appearance | 22 | 0 | C | 0 |
| 3 The equipment should be cleaner | 19 | 2 | 1 | 0 |
| 4 The food should be clearly priced | 6 | 4 | 7 | 5 |

In this example the group consisted of 22 people. You will see that they all wanted more modern equipment to present the food in a better light. They also felt the equipment was dirty (point 3). In fact these two points are related. The old equipment was difficult to keep clean and caused a poor impression to customers. However, they are generally happy with the standard of garnishing but were undecided about how well the prices were displayed. The exercise would be completed for each of the groups of comments that are identified. At the end of the analysis a clear picture of customers' likes and dislikes will emerge.

## 2 Questionnaires

The quality of the data collected using questionnaires is entirely dependent on the design and the questions used. You will, therefore, need to establish your objective: what do you want to achieve, and what do you want to find out about your customers?

An important advantage of a questionnaire is that it makes the data comparable. If 10, 100 or 1000 people are interviewed, using the same questions, the only variable is their response. However the questions must be clearly written so that the researcher asks the same question to everyone and so that it is understood in the same way. Therefore everyday language must be used so that the researcher does not have to prompt or lead the interviewee.

It can be very easy to introduce bias when the questions are written. They can be written in such a way as to get the answer you expect. These are called 'leading questions'. One way to stop this is to use the nominal group technique first. This would bring out the issues and then the questionnaire can be designed afterwards, based on the findings.

You need to consider the length of time it will take to complete each questionnaire. Also, to maintain interest, the questions should be varied and interesting. A link or an explanation may be required between each question to assist this.

The content of the questions will depend on the objective set and the data that is required. There are three areas of data that can be collected:

1 *Fact*. This will cover age, sex, location, social class. It also includes eating out once a month, and which credit cards are used. The question needs to be specific, so if it is about using your facilities you need to qualify the frequency, i.e. choose from once a week, once a month, never.
2 *Opinion*. This includes people's attitudes and feelings. However this data needs careful handling. Asking the question 'Would you use this restaurant?', receiving a 76 per cent 'yes' vote and using that as a sales forecast would be very dangerous. You would need to use a more objective system, such as the Likert scale. This is similar to the nominal group form but it contains a fifth choice, which is 'Neither agree nor disagree'.

The results are analysed in a similar way but statements that are inconclusive are taken out of the process. The statements that are left are those that will best illustrate the respondents' attitudes. The responses are scored on a one to five scale, and thus a final score is achieved which is an average for each statement, based on each respondent's answers. The closer to a score of one the more they agree, the closer to five the more they disagree.

3 *Motive*. If you are looking to influence people's decision-making process, knowing the reasons they do something will be important. It is quite simple to ask 'Why do you use that hotel?' The difficulty is answering that question. It may be that the secretary always books you in there. However, it is not usually as simple as that and there is usually more than one reason. It could be that it is also the closest hotel to your meeting. It is good value for money, the staff are welcoming or the food is good. In order to get a clearer idea of motives it is best to use the nominal group technique or in-depth interviews, which we will discuss shortly.

## What types of question should I ask?

1 *The filter question*. When designing a questionnaire there may well be a need to filter questions based on a specific answer. So, if you ask the question 'Do you use XYZ restaurant?' you must get the answer 'Yes' or 'No'. However, you may then want to find out why they do or do not use the restaurant. The direction then may be:
'If yes, go to Question 2, if no go to Question 3.' This needs to be clear so that questions are not missed out. It is not recommended to use this technique too often as it will become confusing.

2 *Yes/no questions*. I have just used an example of this question: 'Do you use XYZ restaurant?' It is closed and expects the answer 'Yes' or 'No'. These types of questions are easy to ask, easy and quick to answer, and easy to analyse. It is useful to include a 'Don't know' option, so that respondents are not led down one route. This applies more to a question like 'Do you like chilli con carne?' The person may never have tried it and therefore cannot answer 'Yes' or 'No'. Thus the need for the 'Don't know' option.

The three choices should be written down next to the question, so that the chosen answer is simply ringed. This saves time and effort. If the results are being computer analysed then each response can be given a computer code number. This will speed up the process and save time and money.

3 *Multiple-choice question.* At first glance these may seem easy to ask. However, you not only need to know what question to ask but also all the possible answers. You may have been given a multiple-choice question, and thought that your answer does not fit into any of the categories provided. Thus your answer may not reflect your real attitude.

One normally offers the multiple choices available written on a card. The tendency is that the chosen response is more likely to be at the start or at the end. Therefore the choices need to be varied in the order in which they appear, to cancel out this effect.

4 *Open-ended questions.* These are questions that start with 'who', 'what', 'why', 'when', 'where', 'how'. They are very useful in interviews, sales situations and questionnaires that are completed by the respondent. They require more time for completion but will identify attitudes and feelings. However, they will need to be analysed manually, which obviously takes time, and therefore they are not so good on large-scale surveys.

## The importance of presentation

This is particularly important with self-completion questionnaires, yet most hoteliers I have seen use them ignore this point. The questionnaire is on cheap paper, hidden away among the other promotional material, or in the letter rack, sometimes coffee stained!

The result is that they are never filled in. Another reason is that they contain no benefit for the customer. I know that when customers understand the reason for research they are more willing to help. So why don't we put a headline on the questionnaire which reads 'How can we improve the restaurant for your enjoyment? Please help us'?

At least we are now more likely to get the document read. Once it has been read, and if it is easy to fill in, the chances that it will be completed have increased. Time will be an important factor, so ticking boxes will be quicker. However, some people will want to write more, so give them the opportunity. Ask them an open question at the end which allows them to give vent to their feelings, both good and bad.

You also need to make it look important. This will show that you are genuinely interested in the comments. A letter of thanks from the manager would clearly demonstrate an interest in customers' comments. This would also encourage repeat business, yet it never or rarely seems to be done.

The same principles apply if you are doing interview research yourself, so:

1 Write down the introduction, which highlights the customer benefit.
2 Make it easy to follow, give clear instructions to the interviewer, e.g. when to skip questions.
3 Is it easy to fill in, either ticking boxes or providing clipboards?
4 Is the quality of the paper correct for my purpose?
5 Do I have show cards for the various responses to the multiple-choice questions?
6 Thank people for their time and effort.

## Will the questionnaire achieve its objective?

The greatest temptation, once the questionnaire is completed, is to send it out and start the research. It is far better to test it first, to carry out a pilot survey to see if the information that is gathered matches the objective you set at the beginning.

You may consider this time wasting or expensive. However, it is far cheaper to get it right at the start than find out at the end that you have made mistakes.

A pilot survey can be done with just a few interviews. However, you need to note any difficulties that are found in using the questionnaire from the introduction, the responses and the analysis. You may need to ask extra questions such as 'What do you think that question meant?' or 'Why did you make that choice?'

If you try using the questionnaire yourself you will see some of the difficulties that may be encountered. You can then make changes or modifications to eliminate them.

## 3 Research interviews

There are many occasions when you will have the chance to sit down and discuss with customers a variety of matters. It may be about a function, restaurant menu, or accommodation booking. One is always very keen to do this prior to an event, yet far more reluctant afterwards.

Is it a fear of receiving complaints which may require a reduction in the bill that is making you reluctant to interview customers? Or perhaps its importance has not yet occurred to you. If it's the former you have a problem.

You always need to be receptive to customer comments, so when someone comes in to pay the bill why don't you sit down and talk to them? Many of the techniques that apply to questionnaires will apply to the interviews.

The first technique is to establish your objective: what is it you want to find out? Is it why they chose your establishment, how they found the standards of service, or perhaps what other hotels they, their friends, or business colleagues are looking for?

The interview should be structured with questions already written down, to ensure that you achieve the objective. In this situation they need to be open questions so that you identify attitudes and feelings. It may not be appropriate to write down the comments at the time, however the taking down of one or two notes shows interest and concern. A full report can be written up afterwards.

Probing questions are also important. When you receive an

answer it may require clarification. You need to ask a probing question such as 'Tell me more about that incident'; 'You enjoyed the meal, but how did the advice we gave you on the choice of wines help this?'; 'What other factors influenced your choice of location?'

This will take time to master but it will be worth the effort.

## 4 Telephone research

The telephone is a great invention, so use it. Not everyone comes in to pay the bill, so phone them. On the Monday morning after the Saturday evening dinner dance phone and talk to the organizer. They will have received feedback on the night, everything will be fresh in their mind and you can ask questions. It also gives you a great opportunity to book next year's function. This applies to all types of functions, including weddings. It is to be hoped that the same daughter/son will not be getting married again, but they may have brothers, sisters or friends who have just got engaged. If you do not ask, you will never find out.

The telephone can also be used for research, when simple questions that require short answers need to be asked. This is important because your call will have interrupted the person you are talking to and they will want to get back to the work they were doing.

The majority of questions will be 'Do you . . . ?'; 'Don't you . . . ?'; 'Have you . . . ?' or 'Haven't you . . . ?' I used to use the phone to research specific parts of the business, such as Christmas. For instance:

- 'Do you have a Christmas function?'
- 'Do you visit local hotels?'
- 'Have you booked for this Christmas?'
- If no, 'Who is organizing it this year?'

This enabled me to target my Christmas sales activity at those who had not yet made arrangements. If I found that they had already booked, then I made a note to phone earlier next year.

We will look at ways of using the telephone in greater detail in the chapter on Personal Selling (Chapter 12).

## 5 Mail-outs

It is difficult enough taking over a new hotel. On one occasion this was made worse when, on my third day, the hotel's biggest customer reorganized its training schedule for the following year and cancelled £120,000 of business. Needless to say, that left a massive hole.

Some may have said that there was nothing that could be done. We decided to carry out research using a quick and simple questionnaire that identified who used conference facilities, what they required, how often, and the price range they were looking for. We then developed a new conference package based on this information, refurbished the conference facilities by reallocating resources from other projects, and invited all those that replied to the opening of the new facility.

One thousand questionnaires were sent out, 350 were returned and 100 people attended the launch, of which 42 made a reservation of some kind, from accommodation to a conference. The opening ceremony was carried out by the mayor and was featured in all the local media. Personal sales calls were made to every respondent and it meant that all the £120,000 business was replaced with a higher spend than before, which led to an increase in profitability.

The reason for this success was that the questionnaire sent out was easy to complete. When it was received it was possible for respondents to fill it in then and there, rather than leave it for a day or two. We also included a reply-paid envelope so that it could be returned at no cost. Another factor was the accompanying letter which explained our purpose. I stated that we had the opportunity of reviewing all our conference facilities, that we wanted these to match the needs of local businesses, and please could they help. The results speak for themselves, so it is a method I would recommend.

A similar approach could be used by a restaurateur or publican refurbishing facilities or introducing a new menu, or by a hotelier looking to up-grade bedrooms, or a contract caterer wanting to identify why certain sales proposals have been successful.

## 6 Desk research

This is a good starting point for any research programme. It is usually quick and easy to obtain as the information has been produced for some other purpose or person. It takes its name from the type of work that is required, i.e. sitting behind a desk. However, because it has been produced by someone else, it might not always match your requirements. The process of working through a variety of existing sources does have the advantage of familiarizing you with the situation and then generating new ideas. Perhaps it has the greatest use when you are planning to do something new, e.g. launch a new product, manage a new business, move to a new area. It should start by a careful analysis of what information is available. This may require a trip to the library, the local Chamber of Trade or the nearest Tourist Board. Local trade directories, guides and local authority publications can also help. When you have the information, you need to sift through it to ascertain what can be helpful, and therefore you will need to make notes as you go through it.

## 7 Observation

This is such a simple technique but it is too often forgotten or ignored. Observation research can be as simple as watching people walking past the front door of your business. How many stop to read the menu, then make the decision to use the facility? It could be that 1000 people walked past, 100 read the menu and 10 used the restaurant. The fact that the menu display only attracted 10% and that only 1% are enticed in might set alarm bells ringing. We will look at this area again when we look at merchandising (Chapter 13).

## Summary

1 There are two main categories of research – quantative and qualitative.
2 The nominal group technique is very useful in establishing customers' attitudes and in forming the basis of a questionnaire.
3 The successful use of questionnaires depends on how they are designed. Their advantage is that they can be used effectively to compare one respondent with another.
4 You should always aim to gather information, whether it is an informal discussion with a customer or a follow-up call after a function. Keep asking questions.
5 The mailing of questionnaires to potential clients can be used as a sales technique to gather information on a whole range of customer requirements. However, you will need to follow it up with personal sales calls.
6 Desk research uses secondary information and therefore may not precisely fit your needs. However, it is quick, cheap and easier to obtain.
7 Use your eyes to watch what customers do, both inside and outside your business.

## Key questions

1 How much emphasis do you put on researching the attitudes and trends of your customers? Is it sufficient for your future business needs?
2 Which of the techniques suggested will help you develop your business?
3 What are the current attitudes of your customers to your service, and how confident are you that this is a current and accurate situation?
4 How often do you really watch what customers do when they are in or outside your business?

# 5
# Plotting the course: objective setting

We have outlined the current situation in our five case studies, but each picture is far from complete. We have a pencil sketch rather than a finished painting. If we were to start making decisions now based on such sketchy information then we should be guilty of making so many assumptions that our success would be a matter of pure chance. What we need is hard facts upon which to base our plans.

## So what should each of our owners/managers do?

### *The hotel*

There is a definite need to establish all the causes of the poor local reputation. Certainly one of the factors is the high level of labour turnover, however there may be others, e.g. poor decoration and facilities, difficult access, unfriendly staff. The manager might undertake qualitative market research with small groups of local people to find out the relative importance of each of these areas and to ascertain all the points that are contributing to the bad image.

### *The restaurant*

Though only two miles from a major conference town the mainstay of this business is passing trade and local residents, and its proximity to the town does not bring in any significant business. At present the restaurant is quiet mid-week when 85 per cent of the conferences are held. These facts might prompt the manager to carry out a competitor analysis. This would concentrate on those businesses which regularly attract conference delegates to find out why they were successful. Is it that they have special packages which include coach hire? Do they offer private function rooms at no extra charge? Or are there other factors?

The manager could find this out by carrying out desk research. He could phone up and ask for information to be sent to him at a friend's address. This would show what was sent out, how the enquiry was handled, the price offered and any follow-up sales activity used. He might also obtain all the advertising and promotional material from the town's conference office to look at where and how the competitors got their message across to the conference organizers.

## The pub

The landlord could establish the sales and profit contributions of each of his products/services over the last three years. This might show that those aimed at the 50+ age group had accounted for 75 per cent of the profit three years ago but had now fallen to 50 per cent. Was this due to the current economic situation, to a change in the sales mix or to the fact that prices had been kept low to increase volume but had reduced the profit per sale?

This initial research may identify the need to gather more information, such as what would be the current customers' reaction to putting the price up, or why had the younger age groups stopped using the pub so often?

## The staff restaurant

The assistant manager visited a colleague's staff restaurant and saw the different and exciting ways in which they presented their food. She realized that this was a long way from what she was currently offering.

She decided to design a questionnaire and circulate it to a number of office staff to find out what they would like to see improved. When she analysed the results she had a clearer picture, and evidence of what the customers really wanted, to show her boss.

### The fast food restaurant

In the SWOT analysis we identified that one of the opportunities was to start a home delivery service after 6 p.m. Before progressing the idea the manager decided to mail shot a number of potential customers to find out how many would be interested in using the service, what sort of menu they would like and how much they would be prepared to pay for the service.

All the respondents to the mail-out were offered a voucher for £1.00 off their next meal at the restaurant. This had several benefits to the manager:

- He had more information on which to base his decision.
- He had increased awareness of his business.
- A large number of people took up the offer of £1.00 off and became regular customers.

These case studies have several things in common. All were faced with a situation which, if allowed to continue, would cause a decline in their business. They all realized that they needed more information and had set about finding answers to a wide range of questions. This process had proved to all of them that something had to be done. The question is what?

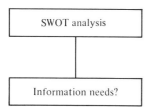

**Figure 5.1**

The information needs should be written down as a list of objectives. These objectives should be quantified because the research results should be assessed against the initial brief.

At this early stage these research objectives are forming the basis of a mini business plan. They are clarifying the manager's thoughts about future action. In our case studies the objectives for finding information may be expressed as follows.

## The hotel

To establish all the factors that contribute to the poor local reputation and to be able to put them in priority order so that they form the basis for future developments.

## The restaurant

To research the needs of conference delegates and quantify the potential market for mid-week, non-residential lunch and dinner business.

## The pub

To find out what would attract the younger generation back to the pub and test customer reaction of the over 50s to increasing the prices by 5 per cent.

## The staff restaurant

To test market the research findings by opening a salad bar, using existing equipment, for a three-month period with the objective of making a 10 per cent contribution to current overheads.

**The fast-food restaurant**

To produce a feasibility study on the setting up of a home delivery service.

These five businesses have now embarked on a programme to find out what is happening in the marketplace, what customers want.

We now explore the framework which will help you to determine the direction you need to move in and to set the objectives you must plan to achieve.

# The framework for the marketing plan

You have now carried out market research and have a clear understanding of your business. You know the size of your markets, the type of customer, the frequency with which they purchase and their attitudes to your hospitality business.

Every effort has been made to exclude your own bias and you are completely customer oriented. You are ready to begin the planning process.

What you have to define now is: where are you going and how do you get there? In other words, set the direction of the business and establish what you are trying to achieve. It is the start of the decision-making process. Once the *direction or the objective* has been set, you then need to look at how you will get there. This second stage will cover the *strategies and tactics* that you need to achieve your final destination and, most importantly, the factors that may limit the development of the new direction.

Objectives, strategy, tactics and limiting factors: what do these words mean, how do we use them to inform the quality of our marketing and how do we balance them within a framework of the planning process?

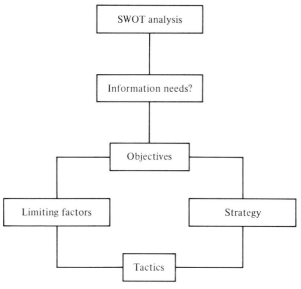

**Figure 5.2**

## Objectives

Objectives should be:

1 *Precise and quantifiable* in terms of sales volume and market share, e.g. to increase sales volume by 5 per cent year on year by increasing market share within a 10-mile radius of 2.5 per cent. This may mean taking business away from competitors if the market is stable in your area. Alternatively you may have seen a new tourist attraction open which has brought new people to the area. In this situation 5 per cent may be a soft option and therefore bad business.

2 *Specific* to particular products, markets or services. So, if the overall objective was to increase sales volume by 5 per cent, this could mean no increase in function business, 10 per cent increase in restaurant food and beverage and 3 per

cent on accommodation. All providing for an overall 5 per cent increase.

3 *Relevant* in the amount of time required to achieve them. It is pointless setting out to achieve something in two years when it cannot be achieved in less than 5 years.

4 *Realistic and achievable* when considering the market trends identified in the research, and the marketing budget that may well have already been set.

5 *Acceptable* to all those that are involved in achieving it. This will ensure their commitment and support. The setting of objectives is therefore a two-way communication process, a team effort that involves middle and senior management.

6 *Measurable.* There is no point in having an objective if it cannot be related to success or failure. Achieving more than we set out to achieve is success, providing it can be sustained. If you failed to reach your target then you need to analyse this: what went wrong and how it can be changed and rectified in the future?

## Strategies

Strategies are the position your business will adopt so that it has the greatest chance of achieving the company objectives. A hotel may have to decide between heavy discounting on price to achieve the maximum number of 'bums in beds'. Alternatively, it could decide to move upmarket with lower occupancy, higher standards of service and food, and higher prices.

The matrix in Figure 5.3 shows the inter-relation between quality, competition, potential and price/profit.

It could be that a five star hotel wants to adopt position B, where it has a high-quality product with low competition and potential but a higher profit margin. Alternatively, you could position a restaurant in position C where it has low quality and price but has high potential and competition. You need to establish where you are on the matrix and then the position of your competition.

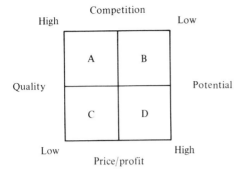

**Figure 5.3**

## Tactics

Tactics are the methods by which you will achieve the strategy. They relate to the use of the tools of the marketing mix and are used to influence and persuade buyers to purchase products and services at the targeted volumes. Tactics include the use of advertising, selling, promotional literature, public relations, direct mail, pricing and discounts. The funding for these marketing tools is scheduled within your plan under the marketing budget. It is the purpose of the marketing plan to help achieve the business objectives.

For instance, a restaurateur has an objective which is:

> To increase profitability from £100,000 to £110,000 by increasing sales 15 per cent overall within the next financial year. This will be made up of increasing food sales by £20,000, lunchtime liquor sales by £4,000, evening food sales by £40,000 and evening liquor sales by £8,000. Food gross profit will be reduced by 5 per cent to reduce prices and thus to attract local chance trade, at an increased level of 15 per cent.

This is a series of quantified objectives, and is specific in terms of products and timespan. What needs to be identified is the strategy and the tactics that will help its achievement. The strategy is hinted at by the commitment to reduce prices and increase volume. Tactics in support of this strategy may then include:

1 Local advertising in free paper once a month.
2 Running a sales promotion each month, promoting value for money.
3 Direct mail to past users of the restaurant.
4 Reprinting and new design for menus.

These tactics can be quantified in cost terms. The number of advertisements is 12 at a cost of £300, totalling £3,600; the cost of promotional material, mailing shots, and design and production of the menus can also be established.

Each tactic, taken from the marketing mix tool-kit, may not only be costed but be subject to its own specific objective.

For instance, the purpose of the advertising campaign may be to increase awareness of the restaurant from, say, 20 per cent to 40 per cent within the distribution area of the free-sheet, the menu may be re-planned to increase spend per head by an average of £1.25 or the mail shot may be aimed at increasing business lunchtime trade by 30 per cent.

There is no point in any marketing tactic if it has no measurable benefit.

The above example is over-simplified in that it ignores whether the restaurant is able to finance the marketing budget. The ability to obtain finance may be limited by the view that head office or the local bank may take of the establishment's prospects. However, the presentation of a coherent marketing and business plan will go a long way to communicate precisely what is to be achieved, and will say a lot about the management's ability to deliver.

Nevertheless, it has to be recognized that any business is bound by constraints and the speed of the development of a business is controlled by external limiting factors, such as the ability to obtain finance for growth or, indeed, working capital.

The following example demonstrates how such limiting factors must be taken into account when laying even the most reasonable of plans.

## Limiting factors and constraints

### *Outside factors/inside factors*

The catering manager of our staff restaurant may want to replace three traditional 'tea-ladies' with a vending service. This may be the most cost-effective solution to what people say they want: a better, more flexible service which is available all day.

However, these employees may be members of a union and the loss of their jobs could have serious industrial relations implications. Thus the ability to effect change may be limited by such an external factor.

Limiting factors can be split into four segments: internal, external, regular and irregular. For the same staff restaurant this split could be applied as shown in Figure 5.4.

The previous example involved a trade union but because it involved a local branch decision it could have been an internal regular factor.

Irregular factors can be just as important. If the catering manager bought the latest and the best piece of kitchen equipment he/she would need to consult not only the head chef but also other key members of the kitchen staff. Failure to do so may limit the successful introduction of that equipment which may, in turn, cause a reduction in productivity or speed of service.

Limiting factors may properly include finance (as we have already discussed), location, car parking, local developments, recruitment and size of premises.

Another factor that may be claimed as limiting is local image and reputation. This is, perhaps, particularly relevant to any catering operation. The cheapest form of advertising is by word of mouth, so a good reputation will mean that customers will talk positively to their friends about your business. However, it is important that you recognize that limiting factors are only admissiable if they really are beyond your control or ability to influence. Image and local reputation are matters you can address, indeed they are the very factors that your marketing, product and quality of service must seek to influence. The need to exploit the excellence of your establishment through good public relations is covered in greater detail in Chapter 10.

| | Regular | Irregular |
|---|---|---|
| Internal | ● Standards of performance manuals<br>● Head chef<br>● Management team<br>● Chief executive and the board<br>● Company policy | ● All levels of staff |
| External | ● Environmental health officers<br>● Trading standards department<br>● Food regulations<br>● Industry codes of practice<br>● Trade unions | ● Customers<br>● Local image and reputation<br>● Standards in the companies' staff restaurants |

**Figure 5.4**

## Summary

1 Objectives must be precise and quantifiable, specific to your products and services, realistic and achievable, acceptable to everyone, measurable and provide a relevant time-span.
2 There is a difference between objectives, strategies and tactics.
3 It is the tactics that will decide how much marketing budget needs to be allocated to achieve the objective.
4 Look at all the factors that can influence and limit your chance of achieving your objective.

## Key questions

1 In what direction is your business heading, and is this right or do you need to change course?
2 Where are you and your competitors situated in the strategic matrix?
3 What limiting factors will affect your achievement of the objective?

# 6

# Product development and test marketing

In the previous chapter our case study examples considered how they might determine a new, positive direction by finding out information that would inform their strategic review. Part of their new strategies would involve the development of new products to both existing and new customers.

Creating any new product or service is a risky business: the skill of the marketeer is to reduce that risk to its minimum by thorough examination of five key areas:

1  research findings,
2  product positioning,
3  test panels,
4  the marketing mix,
5  action plans.

Our case studies set research objectives in the last chapter. How could they now develop and test market the new ideas and concepts that were identified by the research? To help with this we will look at how the five key areas apply to our examples.

But, first, consider the framework shown in Figure 6.1 to assess how these five areas should interact.

*Research findings* inform both *product positioning* and the use of the *marketing mix*. *Test panels*, as we shall see, may be used to check if the products or services are what customers expect and want, and to verify whether the way we promote our products and services through the *marketing mix* is what

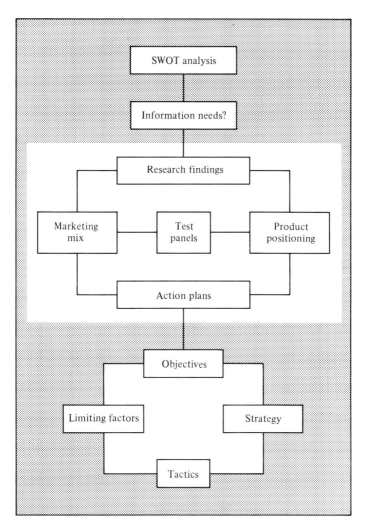

**Figure 6.1**

they anticipate and want. In other words, does what we offer, and what we say we offer, appear credible, desirable and coherent?

*Action plans* are the tools to ensure that we plan in a way which is efficient, effective and monitorable.

*All this activity, properly undertaken, ensures that we have thought through our development strategy and thoroughly tested that strategy so that we can set objectives and progress our marketing plans, confident that they are based on solid, objective knowledge.*

We now revisit the case studies to see how they applied these principles to minimize risk.

# Research findings

As a result of situation analysis, a list of information needs will have generated research into the marketplace, customer attitudes and requirements and, indeed, the way the business itself is perceived.

It would be imprudent to ignore the research results. They may not all be welcome, indeed they may be at variance with your own perceptions, and they may demand much work if they are to be implemented, but the customers have been asked and so are they to be listened to?

## *The pub*

The publican had wanted to find out what would attract the younger generation. He discovered that they wanted more entertainment in the evenings, music nights, karaoke evenings, quizzes and a variety of sporting tournaments.

He was concerned, however, that these events might upset the older generations and he therefore decided to carry out more research to establish what this customer group thought about these ideas. To his pleasant surprise 77 per cent of the older age groups liked the idea of these changes and, of the remainder, 18 per cent said they would still use the pub but on a less regular basis. Only 5 per cent indicated that they would be put off altogether.

The publican was now able to develop the products based on the research findings.

# Product positioning

Chapter 3 considered the customer/service matrix which maps the relationship between competition, quality, market potential and price. With a new product there is an equal requirement to establish where it is positioned on the matrix and its relationship to competitive products.

Research will have shown the likely impact of the development on the business and customers' attitudes towards it as a concept. These results will help to confirm the position of the innovation on the matrix, refine its development, and contribute to the design and accurate, effective targeting of the promotional plan.

### *The restaurant*

Our restaurant manager undertook research into the requirements of the conference market. He discovered that a clear majority of conference organizers reported that delegates were happy to spend less per head on food but anticipated relatively high expenditure on liquor. They tended to stay in town to avoid drinking and driving. The research also showed that while they usually occupied several tables in the restaurant, ideally they would prefer a private function room.

The restaurateur decided to re-position his conference dinner package at a higher price but to include some new features:

● Free transport from the hotel to the restaurant and return to the hotel.
● A private room for parties of 15 or more.
● A complimentary liqueur at the end of the meal.

The restaurant had, therefore, re-positioned itself against its competitors. It had increased its price but had also improved the value for money and service it offered. It was now a question of promoting the new package and showing how it was different from, and better value against, the competition.

## Test panels

'I told you it would not work.' This is the typical reaction of the negative person who can't wait to pour cold water on every new idea. To reduce the risk of failure to its minimum you need to test market the new product.

This should include producing the new product and then giving it to existing and potential customers, management and staff to try. This could be done by setting up a test panel of these people and asking for their opinions and attitudes to the new product. It might be a question of tasting the proposed food and wine, or it could be to gauge their reaction to the promotional material you are going to use or their ideas about the refurbishment programme.

Their comments are a vital sounding board, and if you get negative feedback then you will need to widen the research and confirm those findings. Listen to the comments, ask more questions, carry out further research, make changes as a result, then re-submit the ideas to the panel. When they give you positive feedback, you are ready to launch. This method reduces the risk element to a minimum.

### The staff restaurant

The assistant catering manager in our staff restaurant is introducing a new salad bar. She is, however, unsure what items should be on the menu so sets up a series of test panels recruited from office staff and shop-floor workers. A number of dishes and salads were tried and marked out of ten. The most popular ones were to be incorporated into the new menu. The benefit was two-fold: she found out which were the most popular dishes, and staff involvement on the test panels created advance publicity and interest.

## The marketing mix

You may have come across this term before. It is often described as the 'four Ps', but with the rapid emergence of environmental issues a fifth P is growing in importance. The marketing mix covers:

- Product,
- Price,
- Place,
- Promotion,
- Planet.

We will look at price and promotion later, but how would our case study hotelier consider product and place? You may remember that he had a poor local reputation and his research objective was to find out why.

### *The hotel*

The research may highlight a variety of shortcomings in the operational standards of the hotel. For instance:

*The product*
1  the quality and freshness of the food,
2  the speed and style of service,
3  the choice of dishes available,
4  the daily variety,
5  the equipment used, e.g. cutlery and china,
6  the quality of presentation of the food,
7  the times of service, e.g. Monday to Friday 12 noon to 2 p.m.,
8  the friendliness of staff,
9  the appearance and professionalism of the staff.

*The place*
1  the décor, inside and out,
2  the standard and quality of furnishings,

3 the appearance of the menu and other merchandising displays,
4 directional signs,
5 access and location,
6 warm and welcoming,
7 cleanliness of facilities.

It is now for the manager to decide how to develop his product and place to meet the customers' requirements. Clearly this has to be done before promotion and price may be addressed for the hotel as a whole. Some of these areas may cost money but many are low-cost schemes that may be implemented quickly, e.g. staff training, and new menu displays.

The extra P in the marketing mix stands for 'Planet'. This is because of the enormous change in people's attitude towards the environment which was started with a number of pressure groups such as Greenpeace and Friends of the Earth. Consumers now demand, and purchase in ever-increasing quantities, those products that take more care of the world's future. So far this has not really had an effect on the industry, but the situation will change, with more and more customers wanting to know your policy on:

● Purchasing and the environmental checks that you make on suppliers.
● Packaging and the efforts you have made to reduce it, e.g. moving away from individually packaged items to bulk portions.
● Recycling and what efforts you make to collect waste and return it for future use, e.g. cans, bottles, paper.
● Energy conservation and how you ensure energy wastage is eliminated, e.g. monitoring heating.
● Health and safety, and the types of cleaning materials used and their effect on the environment.
● Transport and how you reduce the use of company cars, purchase unleaded petrol or catalytic converters.
● The use of recycled paper for all stationery and print material (the quality of this paper is improving all the time).

- Equipment – the energy efficiency of new equipment will become more important – as well as how you dispose of old equipment, e.g. fridges.
- The use of organic food.

This is not an exhaustive list and the situation and emphasis will change in the future as the environmental issues alter in importance. You could ignore this area and wait until you are forced to take action by central government, but it is reasonable to assume that more and more customers will be asking about your policy on a range of environmental issues.

### The fast-food restaurant

Our fast-food restaurant, you will remember, was under pressure because of litter on the pavement outside the outlet. It would be a simple process to correct this if the manager was really serious about the environment.

His starting point would be to carry out an environmental audit, the purpose of which is to establish the full range of key issues.

These may include his purchasing policy and the policy of suppliers, packaging and the efforts to reduce wastage and litter.

Consider again the check-list. Which of the issues may apply to this case study? Can you add to the list?

## Action plans

Each of our case study managers needs to create an action plan because new products or product changes do not simply happen, they have to be properly managed. Each requires careful planning, continuous reassessment, additional changes and developments.

This pocket book does not support the theory 'that looks like a good idea, so let's do it'. It proposes the need for the same careful planning that is invested in the overall business plan. This will be further discussed in Chapter 17. At this stage we need to agree that an action plan is not just a list of actions to be taken (see Figure 6.2). It must include:

1 the action required,
2 the key tasks or stages,
3 who will be responsible,
4 when it should be completed by,
5 a section for review and update.

The action plan needs to be formalized and agreed with all parties so that they are all committed to its achievement.

| Action required: | | | |
|---|---|---|---|
| Key tasks | By whom | Completion target date | Comments and reviewed by |
| | | | |
| | | | |
| | | | |
| | | | |
| | | | |
| | | | |
| | | | |
| Action completed: | | | |

**Figure 6.2**

## Summary

1 Launching new products is a risky business, however this risk can be considerably reduced.
2 Establish where you and your competitors fit into the customer/service matrix so that you know if, and how, to differentiate your product from that of your competitors.
3 Use all the available research to develop your product. If there are gaps in the information make sure they are filled.

4  Assess all the five Ps. Product and place are to do with operational standards. Be aware of the growing importance of the fifth P, the planet.
5  Create test panels and listen to their comments. Reassess the product in the light of their ideas and then make further changes to the product, until you have gained the confidence to proceed.
6  A complete product development and launch does not just happen. It needs careful organization and planning.

## Key questions

1  What new products have you developed in the last two years?
2  How successful have they been?
3  How could this have been improved?
4  What importance will the fifth P, the planet, have on the future of your business?
5  Who could you invite to be on a test panel?

# 7
## Is the price right?

Establishing the right pricing policy for all facets of the business is a critical strategic decision. The price you set for your products or services makes a major statement about how you wish those products and services to be perceived by your customers.

Pricing policy will be an essential part of the confirmation of your new direction; it will be a key factor in the way products may be developed and it will be an essential ingredient in your selection of the marketing mix as part of your new image.

Of course the relationship between the price of a product and what it costs to produce is critical, but the one question you should bear in mind as you read this chapter is just how much has the way you set your price got to do with cost?

Cost and price are two very different aspects of your business. Costs are totally within your control. They are based on how careful the head chef is about food wastage, how diligent the housekeeping staff are about turning lights and heating off, or the way in which restaurant staff control the use of table laundry. You may be involved in negotiating with local suppliers on a regular basis, always looking for the best deals. It all adds up to the fact that, dependent on the size of your business and its purchasing power, the costs of letting a room or serving a meal are controlled by you and your management team.

You may currently believe that you have the same control over price. You may well be the person who sets the price of the table d'hôte menu or the single room, but there are a number of factors that will have influenced your final decision. It might have been based on company policy and the need to make a 65 per cent food gross profit, or the fact that the competitors down the road have just put their prices up. These are internal and external price factors, which we will look at again below.

## The factors that influence price

There are two types of factor that influence price. These are internal and external and in their simplest form cover the following areas:

1 *Internal factors*
   ● how much does it cost to produce the products?
   ● what return do you want to make?
2 *External factors*
   ● the demand for your products,
   ● the state of the marketplace,
   ● what the competition is doing.

### Internal factors

You should know what it is costing to produce each of your products. If you don't then you need to establish the costs now because, for all you know, you could be selling some products at a loss. There are two types of cost to be included – fixed and variable.

The fixed costs still have to be paid whether you have nobody or a hundred people buying the product. They include costs like business rates and insurances. Variable costs can go up or down according to the number of people using the product, e.g. laundry, food and heating.

Once you have the costs, ask yourself what sort of return you want to make. Is it 65 per cent on food, 60 per cent on liquor and 90 per cent on rooms, or is it different? It may be that there are company guidelines on the return that is expected. If that is the case it is easy to use those percentages, or perhaps it is based on past experience of the industry. However, whatever method is used, it must not be taken in isolation and at the expense of external factors.

## External factors

You have less control over these factors because they are the outside influences on the particular marketplace that your products are in. For example, the state of the marketplace will depend on action taken by the government to control inflation or reduce unemployment. It could also be subject to events taking place in other parts of the world which may affect the economy, or the economic prospects of one of your major business customers.

Demand will also vary according to other factors. An obvious example is seasonal variation. Holiday hotels are busier in the summer; function hotels are busier in the winter. Another factor may be the pattern of trade: staff restaurants may have a higher demand on different days of the week that fall into a regular pattern. Public houses may have a monthly variation on the demand for their product.

Let us look at the effects of demand and price for a three-star seaside hotel. There will be a very good case to have varying prices not only for different times of the year but for the different types of room. So a room with a sea view will demand a higher price because more people want that type of room, rather than one overlooking the town. However, that demand might be very high between July and September and very low from December to February. Therefore, in the quieter months you would need to consider possible seasonal tariffs according to the demand for the different types of room. In summer you would consider charging a premium price for the sea-view room. One word of caution about these price variations, the staff selling the accommodation must be trained to understand how and when these variations in tariffs apply – and be trained to 'sell up', that is to persuade customers to purchase the higher priced rooms by selling the benefits to them.

The final external factor is the competition. What are they doing? Are they putting prices up or down, offering added value in the form of sales promotions, direct mailing to your existing customers, or something else? Just how important is price in providing the competitive edge? Is a price promotion the most effective way of combating the competition or is it more effective to promote more creatively by offering enhanced value packages?

Remember that nobody buys on price alone and it is fatal to allow strategic or tactical marketing to be dominated by price considerations. This point having been made, it must be appreciated that you are in a price sensitive industry. You will have had the complaint from a customer about a bottle of wine costing £7.95 when it can be bought from the local supermarket for £2.95, or the comment in the bar about 2p on a pint when the pub down the road only put on 1p. Such comments may be easily answered, directly or simply by the service and environment of the establishment. But what of the other side of this picture? What happens if your prices are perceived as low?

## Price makes a statement about your business

The owner/manager of a 16-bedroom hotel in the east Midlands was lucky to get crucial feedback from a business customer one morning.

The customer had checked in late the previous evening, his secretary having made the reservation by phone at 5.30 p.m. As he settled the bill, he remarked on how comfortable he had been and what good value the hotel gave. 'In fact', he went on to say, 'I'm not altogether sure you're not letting yourself down.'

'I beg your pardon, sir', exclaimed the surprised owner, 'but in what way?'

'Let me explain,' the customer said. 'I normally stay in an hotel down the road but yesterday I had to make a last minute journey over here and they were fully booked. Quite genuine: they'd have fitted me in if they possibly could have and in fact they offered to ring round and get me in somewhere else local. My secretary decided to do the job herself – she knows what I like if you know what I mean – and so she pulled out the guides and got on with it. Had one helluva job, must be some show on around here or something. Anyhow, by the time she got down the list to this place, if you'll forgive me, she was getting absolutely spare, so when you or someone said there was a room, en-suite and all that, she was one hell of a relieved girl. I mean by this time it was well after 5.15 and all she wanted to do was get me on the carphone, tell me where I could rest my weary little head and scarper off home. And then it nearly all fell apart when you confirmed the room rate at £34.50 including full English breakfast. At that point she nearly put the phone down, got on to me and suggested a rapid divert back to Coventry.'

'But why? What was wrong?'

'I'll tell you what was wrong, and it'll be the best bit of unpaid, unsolicited consultancy you're likely to get all year, and don't worry, I won't ask for an extra discount for services rendered. I reckon with this bill I've had more than my money's worth – almost feel embarrassed to settle it with the company plastic.

'No, you see, the point is about a fortnight ago I stayed in another place, somewhere in Blackburn it was, another last minute arrangement, and that room in that so-called hotel was charged at £36 all-in, colour telly, the lot. The only trouble was that most of the kit, including the telly and the teasmade, was US and the room was filthy, spent most of the night trying to work out the most hygienic route to the toilet. Not very pleasant and definitely not to be repeated as I politely advised my secretary, not that she's to blame, don't think she's been further north than the proverbial Watford Gap.

'So, you see, when she heard what you charged she naturally assumed the worst. Frankly, if it hadn't been for the way you managed to reassure her over the phone, I wouldn't be here now giving you this slice of advice.

'Which is, bluntly, put your prices up and stop giving the wrong impression. I'm no expert but I stay in lots of hotels all round this country and by my reckoning you've got to be in the £40–45 bracket, no trouble, and people like me will be confident to book and more than happy to pay your bill. You've got a really neat place here. Good morning!'

The same lesson would apply to someone booking a wedding reception. If they wanted to ensure a trouble-free reception, with high-quality food, wines and service, they may be more than happy to pay top of the range prices. However, if they decided on their local restaurant, they will not only expect to pay less but accept a lower level of food and service quality. They are not saying this quality is unacceptable, just that when all the factors are considered, it represents the best value for their particular needs.

In both these examples price is making a statement about the business. The higher the price then the higher the customer's expectations of quality and service. As the price comes down then so will the customer's expectations decrease. Not everyone wants the finest standards and the prices that accompany this. The price you offer must match the standards of food and service that you set, and reflect the customer expectations. You can be both too cheap and too expensive, so ensure that the price you charge makes the right statement about the quality of your business.

## Strategic and tactical pricing

Price can be used strategically. It could be used to:

1  Keep price the same to maintain market share.
2  Reduce price to increase volume.
3  Increase prices to achieve higher profits with relatively lower costs.
4  Introduce a new product at a very competitive price to ensure a high penetration of the marketplace (this would be too dangerous for small companies because it could stretch financial resources).
5  Introduce a higher value new product to achieve an early return on the initial investment.

6 Start with price parity with the competition but add value
to your product.

The following case study examples demonstrate how price
promotions may be used strategically – to reinforce the new
direction, quality and image – and tactically – to smooth out
peaks and troughs, and to open up new business
opportunities.

We already know that the restaurateur had decided to re-
position his conference dinner package and that part of the
way in which this was presented was to offer an enhanced
package at a higher price.

The new service obviously should cost more but the higher
charges may well attract business because the business
customer may perceive that this stands for professionalism
and quality.

## The hotel

Reduced the winter weekend break price from £40 per guest
per night full board to £35 for the quieter period between
January and March.

## The pub

Introduced 'Happy Hour' with doubles at single prices to
increase early evening trade and to capture customers who
stay on longer.

## The fast-food restaurant

Charged a higher price for home delivery after 6 p.m.

Higher charge justified by added convenience – saves time
and cost of preparing evening meal and therefore represents
higher value.

### *The staff restaurant*

Prices maintained at old levels despite wider range of sandwiches, offering better choice than the competition.

Deliberately absorbed VAT increase to show faith and only began to apply selective price increases on certain items once market share had increased by 25 per cent.

## Summary

1 You have complete control over costs but you don't have the same control on price.
2 Beware of under-pricing your products.
3 There are both internal and external factors that will affect your final decision on price.
4 Nobody buys on price alone, there are many other considerations that influence customers' final purchase.
5 However, this is a price-sensitive industry.
6 Price makes a statement about the standards and quality of your business.
7 Pricing can be used in a variety of ways to obtain strategic advantage.
8 Be very careful when competitors reduce their price – consider keeping yours static or increasing them rather than starting a price war.

## Key questions

1 What are the real costs of each of your products?
2 What are the current internal and external factors? What effect are these having on your pricing policy?
3 What factors, apart from price, affect your customers' purchase decision?
4 Does your pricing strategy make the right statement about the quality of your business, or are you over- or under-priced?

5 Which, if any, of the pricing strategies could help you develop your business?
6 What would you do if your main competitor put their prices up?

# 8
# The promotional mix

This chapter explains the promotional mix, how it should be employed and the objectives it should achieve. Its application is an essential part of marketing because it specifies what, how and when we are to communicate with the customer. It is, in effect, the tactical tool-kit.

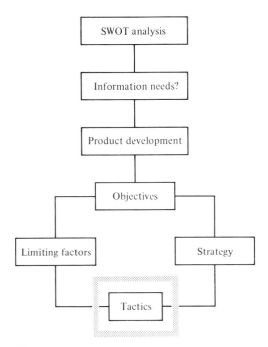

**Figure 8.1**

The promotional mix covers five key areas which will be explained in the following chapters. They are:

1 *Advertising*. This is producing paid for, controlled messages which are targeted at large numbers of people within a short space of time.
2 *Sales promotion*. Techniques that encourage customers to purchase by providing added value to the products that are promoted.
3 *Public relations*. A planned and sustained effort that maintains goodwill and mutual understanding between an organization and its publics.
4 *Direct mail*. A personalized communication which provides existing and prospective customers with the chance to respond directly.
5 *Personal selling*. A personal presentation of your products to either existing or potential customers.

The purpose of these promotional tools is to communicate with potential and existing customers. Too often, the existing customers are forgotten. They use your business already, they know of your product and, more often than not, they have extra business to give you. They are also 'sales' people, a surrogate salesforce, who will use 'word-of-mouth' both to promote and criticize your business.

The promotional mix is concerned with getting messages across to customers about your business. It could be described as message management. Some of these messages can be very precisely targeted, others less so. However, they provide you with a range of tactics that will enable you to achieve your objectives.

## Identification of resources

With each of these components of the promotional mix you have the choice of doing it yourself or buying in the service. Obviously, if you buy in it is going to be more expensive. However if you first review what you have available, you may identify new resources. In my experience many management and staff have hidden talents which, when developed, enhance the business and the motivation of all concerned.

I remember entering a hotel Christmas competition and wondering what to do. When we brought the team together we identified an assistant manager with great creative skills for producing posters, a part-time member of staff who was brilliant at writing copy for the various brochures, a waitress who came up with excellent ideas on how to decorate the hotel, and I found a talent for impersonating a jolly gentleman with a white beard and red coat!

## Identification of customer target groups

Before we look at the components of the promotional mix in detail, two pieces of advice:

1 identify the target audience, precisely,
2 keep the message simple.

One approach to targeting could be to load up an old-fashioned blunderbus with all your promotional activity. When you point it at the target, fire it. The promotions scatter over a wide area. The difficulty is that only some of them will reach the people they were intended for. You need to identify more clearly who you are trying to talk to – so that it is more like using a rifle.

The other point is simplicity. Too often one sees elaborate promotional material that is never read. If it is never read, your message can never be understood and acted on. The simpler and easier that message is to receive, the more it will be read and the greater your chance of success.

In the next few chapters we will look at technique. To enable you to understand more about the various techniques we will look at the situation behind the scenes. We will examine how advertising is created by an agency, the various types of sales promotion, the tricks of the public relations business, techniques of direct mail and how successful sales people operate. One important rule applies to every promotional initiative: it must have a purpose that conforms to and supports the overall marketing strategy.

## Promotional objectives

The broad purpose of any promotional activity is to inform, persuade and remind. However, you need to be as specific as possible, working to clear promotional objectives. Some examples of objectives are:

1 To build awareness of the hospitality product and its organization.
2 To highlight differences between your business and your competitors.
3 To show the benefits of using your particular hospitality offering.
4 To persuade a particular group of potential customers to use your business.
5 To maintain the reputation and business.
6 To generate enquiries for brochures and other promotional literature.
7 To develop and increase brand loyalty so that existing customers purchase more frequently.
8 To change attitudes towards your business within the local area.

These are still fairly broad objectives. If we look at our case study examples we now know enough about their situation and what they want to achieve to suggest specific promotional objectives for them.

### The hotel

To change attitudes within the immediate marketplace (within a seven-mile radius) so that at least 50 per cent of people surveyed place the hotel as number one in terms of quality of food, accommodation and friendliness of welcome.

### The restaurant

To achieve 45 per cent awareness among conference organizers visiting the area of the existence and value of the special
dinner conference package.

### The pub

To persuade at least 10 per cent of the local 18–25 age group
to visit the pub on at least one of its new 'Music Nights'
within the first three months.

### The staff restaurant

To communicate the benefits of a healthy diet to the entire
workforce through the provision of a new salad bar and to
increase sales by £400 per week by month 3.

### The fast-food restaurant

To create awareness among 60 per cent of households within
the town of the new after 6 p.m. home delivery service, and to
achieve 500 home sales by week 8.

## Summary

1 The promotional mix involves advertising, personal selling,
  sales promotion, public relations and direct mail. They are
  your tactics.
2 Their purpose is to communicate your product messages to
  both existing and potential customers.
3 Before deciding on the tactics, set a promotional
  objective.
4 You have many resources in your business – identify them
  and use them.

5 Your messages need to be targeted precisely, and if kept simple are more likely to succeed.

## Key questions

1 What is your promotional objective?
2 Which promotional tactics are best suited to achieve this objective?
3 What resources can you identify within your business to assist the promotional objective?

# 9
# Advertising

We are all subject to the influences of advertising. It confronts us in every part of our daily life, reading newspapers, listening to the radio, driving to work (through posters), watching television or going out to the cinema. It is a multi-million pound business, but why do people advertise, what is advertising and how are ads created?

## Why does any business advertise?

There are many reasons, here are some of them.

1 To announce a new reason for buying now, e.g. reduced price or added value.
2 To encourage an impulse purchase.
3 To create awareness.
4 To promote a good impression of the product.
5 To show how your product is different from the competitors'.
6 To show your product is better than the competitors'.
7 To counter activity from competitors.
8 To encourage recognition of the company.
9 To create customer loyalty.
10 To establish a new product in the marketplace.
11 To maintain existing customer usage.
12 To increase existing customer usage.
13 To persuade potential customers to write for a brochure or phone for more information.

## Why would our five case studies want to advertise?

### The hotel

1 To inform past customers that the hotel is now under new management in order to change the old reputation.
2 To create customer awareness that the refurbishment programme has been completed in the restaurant.

### The pub

1 To inform customers of forthcoming musical attractions in the evening.
2 To show the greater variety of musical events available against the competition.

### The restaurant

1 To persuade conference organizers to phone for a menu and brochure on the new conference package.
2 To promote an image of the family weekend place to visit for a restaurant meal or bar snack.

### The fast-food restaurant

1 To launch the new home delivery service with a special price promotion.
2 To inform customers how and where to get the new delivery service.

### The staff restaurant

1 To promote the healthy qualities of the new salad bar menu.
2 To increase the frequency of current customer usage.

# The process of advertising

Whether you use a third-party, such as an advertising agency, or whether you plan to produce the advertising yourself, there are three key steps which involve careful and considered decisions.

1 Objectives: what must the advertisement achieve?
2 The image: what message does the advertising convey?
3 The medium: press, television, posters, or what?

The key question is how to get the most effective advertising within your budget.

## Step one: the objective

The first step is to set the advertising objective. In the next few chapters we will look at setting promotional objectives for advertising, PR, sales promotion, direct mail and personal selling. Every one of these objectives must support the overall objectives of the business set out in your marketing plan. In this way you will create a hierarchy of objectives with which to build your business.

Our case studies have identified why they want to advertise; now let's look at how they quantify what they want to achieve.

### *The hotel*

To generate 400 local lunch and dinner customers per week for the newly refurbished restaurant within one month of opening.

### *The pub*

To increase evening liquor sales by 10 per cent between 7.30 p.m. and closing time on all 'Music Nights'.

### The restaurant

To generate 40 enquiries per month for the new 'Conference Dinner' package over the next three months.

### The fast-food restaurant

To establish the new home delivery service and for 100 customers to use the price promotion coupon within the first month.

### The staff restaurant

To increase current customer usage from 2.4 times per week to 3 times.

## Step two: the brief

The next stage is to write the brief for the agency or whoever is producing the ad. The best brief would be a copy of your business plan. However, in the early stages this may be difficult. Another way is to consider four key questions which will clarify your thought process.

1 Who is my message aimed at?
2 What message do I want to get across?
3 How can I support the claim I am making?
4 What lasting impression do I want to create?

The first question concentrates on the target audience. There are several ways of identifying this group. It can be done using a classification which establishes the type of house they live in (ACORN: a national survey based on the census of the population). Another method is to split the population into five socio-economic groupings or even by psychological type. If these areas of marketing interest you, you will find more information in other, more specialized, marketing books.

   This book proposes a simpler method and that is to

visualize the target audience. But how do you visualize a customer?

Let us return to our hotelier. He has already carried out research into the perceptions and attitudes of his local customers. Since he arrived at the hotel he has got to know a number of people who currently use the restaurant. Through his involvement with local organizations he has also spoken to a number of customers who stopped using the facility. Due to his research he has a clear picture of the person he wants to attract.

As, for instance, the potential customer or target audience may be described as: Mr and Mrs Jones, aged 55 and 52 respectively. Mr Jones is a middle manager in a local factory and his wife has just got a part-time job for 15 hours per week in the doctor's surgery. They live on the side of town which has more detached and semi-detached houses, although their house is a three-bedroom bungalow. There are two children, one of whom has just married and moved about 50 miles away; the other is at university. Mr and Mrs Jones eat out at least once a week. Each month they take two friends out for a bar snack on a Sunday. They also go out for birthdays and other anniversaries, or when their family visit. Mr Jones is a member of the golf club and a governor of the local primary school. Mrs Jones is a member of the WI and local drama group.

The hotelier, having visualized this target audience, now needs to establish what message he wants to get across. This might be: 'Freshly prepared, good quality food, served by friendly staff in pleasant surroundings.'

How can this claim be supported? This could be achieved by the use of a picture of the new restaurant together with a quote from a happy, satisfied customer, or an extract from a local newspaper report or hotel guide.

What final impression should be created? In this case the final impression should demonstrate that the hotel, with its new, fresh, quality image, is very different now from what it was before the new manager arrived.

The brief *can* now be used to inform the creation of the ad.

## Step three: production

The job has not yet finished. You will need to check the final ad to see if it works. One method is to use the AIDA test. AIDA is an acronym that stands for:

- *A*ttention
- *I*nterest
- *D*esire
- Action.

You will need to consider whether or not it gains the reader's attention. Imagine it among many other ads. Would it stand out against them?

If it has gained attention, do they want to read on? If nobody reads it then your message can never be communicated.

Once they have read it, does it create desire for the product or service? Does it create sufficient desire so that Mr Jones picks up the phone and makes a booking in the new restaurant?

It may be very difficult for you to be totally objective about this analysis, especially if you have been heavily involved in its creation. However, you will have many friends and local customers who can give you constructive criticism. Ask them and listen to their comments.

Another way of applying objectivity is to analyse other people's ads using the AIDA principle. Which ads in your local paper or on television have attracted your attention and then prompted you to take action? Ask yourself what caught your eye and what appealed to you about them.

## The agency could also be you

You may decide to employ an advertising agency or you may choose to do it yourself. But what are the various advantages and disadvantages? They are described in Tables 9.1 and 9.2.

**Table 9.1**  The agency option

| Advantages | Disadvantages |
|---|---|
| They provide a complete service with all-round expertise. | They do not have a detailed knowledge of either your business or your industry. |
| They will be more objective because they are an outsider looking in. | They are more expensive because they are doing more work, however this saves you time and worry. |
| They will manage the whole process. | They have other clients and not all their time will be devoted to your needs. |
| When you work with the same agency for a period of time they will provide greater benefit as they understand your business. | The smaller your account the more likely they are to be less effective. |

**Table 9.2**  Do it yourself

| Advantages | Disadvantages |
|---|---|
| You retain complete control over the process. | It is very easy to make mistakes. |
| You have a greater understanding of your business and your industry. | You are less likely to have all the skills to undertake the work. |
| It can be faster and is always cheaper. | Your own bias may cloud your judgement. |

You may enjoy learning as you go.

Whichever you choose it is useful to know how an agency works. Whatever the size of the company you are dealing with, there are four basic functions that companies undertake. The smaller the agency the greater the likelihood that two or more of the functions will be carried out by the same person.

The functions are:

- account management,
- creativity,
- media buying,
- traffic and production.

Account managers are really the sales function, providing a link between you and the agency. They may discuss the brief with you and agree the various time schedules required.

The creative people come up with the ideas on how your message is communicated. This may cover a combination of sound, pictures, words and colours, depending on the media being used.

The media buyer selects and purchases the time slots or pages for you, the client. They should agree with you when and where the ad will appear and then purchase space for the ad at the most favourable terms.

Traffic and production take the creative idea and turn it into a final piece of artwork, a radio broadcast or a TV ad.

If you have decided to take on this role and do it yourself, then be aware that there is an increasing amount of help available from the various parts of the media. Local papers, who rely heavily on local advertising, have had their own creative people for a long time. We are now seeing more and more help being given to the smaller business by commercial radio and television. Give them a ring and see what is available to you.

## Step four: which medium?

Which will be the most cost-effective of the media for your advertisements? Consider their relative strengths and weaknesses.

### Television

This reaches a large audience. It is a very impactive medium as it uses both colour and sound. You may not be able to afford or want national coverage, however a local commercial TV company may be a possibility. The difficulty is that although it reaches many people, it is not selective in its views. Production costs can also be high but this can be reduced by using still photographs and a voice-over.

## The press

Local and national newspapers are read by interested people; they have decided to buy that newspaper or have it delivered. You can control the type of person reading your ad by the paper you chose to place it in. Our hotelier will interest certain types of holiday-maker by advertising in the *Daily Mail* that he could not attract if he used the *Sun*.

## Commercial local radio

This media has grown rapidly over the last 10 years and it is set to continue. The creative use of sound, voice and music enables ads to be impactful. They can be repeated regularly at low cost and they are relatively cheap to produce. The drawback is that most people have the radio on as background noise to accompany household chores or driving. The listener is not always concentrating on the broadcast and effective use of this medium may depend on heavyweight, frequent repeats.

## Magazines and journals

These usually have a specific and specialist type of reader. Although they have a relatively low circulation compared to newspapers, they have a higher readership – that is one person buying it but more people reading it. A major difficulty is that they may have a longer lead time – this is the time between placing the ad and when it is actually printed.

## Outdoor advertising

Large poster sites can be effective, however for the smaller business they are impractical. Unless many sites are used the initial print and production costs are prohibitively high. However there are many opportunities to use A2-sized posters both inside and outside your business. They should be positioned where potential customers are likely to see them. Our staff restaurant could have announced the opening of the new salad bar by placing posters in the lifts and reception areas.

## Theatres and cinemas

The cinema can be very effective if you want to attract the under 30s. The big screen brings everything to life. However, like television, the costs are higher, especially with each cinema needing its own copy. Theatres often use 35 mm slides for projection in the interval, as well as having ads in the programme.

## Directories and guides

An increasing number of hotel and restaurant guides are competing for space on booksellers' shelves. There have also been a number of cases where bogus guides have been promoted and money obtained from hoteliers but the publication never produced. Always ask to see the previous edition and check where it is sold. Guides can be useful provided you plan your activity.

The most widely available directory is *Yellow Pages* and its use is promoted using television. Your entry can be enhanced from a single line to semi-display or display, with prices starting at £70. However, you might want to consider placing entries under different headings. Our hotelier might place an entry under 'Hotels, Restaurants and Weddings' to advertise the different services available.

## Some points to consider

We have now looked at the three parts that make up the world of advertising.

There are no hard and fast rules that will make your advertising successful. However, there are some pointers that we can pass on. They are based on experience, market research and the workings of the human eye. These points will apply to ads, brochures and all other types of print material that you create.

1   It is not what it is, it is what it does. When you look at your local paper, look at how many ads promote the features of the business (what it is), rather than the benefits (what it does). You must always promote the customer benefits. Let's look at some examples within our case studies.

**Table 9.3**

| Features | Benefits |
| --- | --- |
| 30 rooms with private bath. | Relax in a comfortable bedroom with your own en-suite facilities. |
| Bar snacks available. | Good value meals. |
| Weekly music nights. | A great night out. |
| 200 seats. | Plenty of room available. |
| High-street location. | Within easy walking distance of shops. |

The importance of promoting the benefits will be expanded in the chapter on Personal Selling.

2   Use the customers' language. You may believe we all speak the same language. We generally do, however we all have our own jargon and slang. For example, in the

hospitality industry we have different meanings for station, chance and covers.

One of the most difficult groups to talk to is children. The language they use is always changing, almost as fast as the 'top ten'. I was discussing this difficulty with a major supplier and telling him the difficulty I had with the word 'groovy'. I thought it meant the 'in' thing and I had prepared a promotion about 'Groovy Grub'. At the last minute I realized that I had not tested this on potential customers. This was carried out and I discovered that 'groovy' had a new meaning. It now related to when it *was* in fashion, and that was some time ago. Thus its new meaning was 'outdated and old fashioned'. The supplier had been very quiet and I asked what the matter was. It turned out that he had gone to watch his son play rugby the previous Saturday and as his son ran out on to the pitch he shouted, 'They're a groovy pair of jeans, Dad.' The supplier then added 'Until now I thought that was a compliment!'

Ensure you use simple language that the customer uses regularly and therefore understands.

3 Choose the right typeface. Too often we take the use of typefaces for granted or leave it to the printer – don't! Different typefaces create different images. You may need to use a test panel to decide which is the right typeface for your customers. You should use a serif type, which is the one with the little flicks at the bottom of each letter. This creates a line for the eye to work along and thus it is easier to read. The quality images are better with a serif typeface, e.g. if you look at the daily newspapers, the quality papers use a serif while the tabloids do not.

4 Use pictures of finished dishes rather than raw ingredients. Market research has shown that customers are more likely to buy if they see a picture of the final dish rather than its raw ingredients. So use those pictures.

5 Create an image. The name you use for your business is

very important. How you get that name across is even more so. You need to create your own style and then use it on all occasions.

For example, our hotelier decided to create his own logo which showed a pencil drawing of the hotel frontage with the name underneath. He wanted to promote the idea of good and friendly service to overcome the old images. He therefore added 'Always making you welcome'. He made this his logo and used it on all brochures, menus, letters, ads, etc. When customers saw it they started to establish the name and message in their minds. Over a period of time this recognition and message would grow stronger provided he always kept the picture, words, typeface and message the same.

6 Check the copy: the text in the ad. Any error in any printed material is unforgivable. You must double check any copy before it goes to the printer. If you want to check spellings then read the copy backwards. This slows your reading speed down and makes you look at each word more carefully. You should also get a second opinion and ask someone else to read it.

7 Third-party advertising. In this industry we often sell services to one party who then sells them again as part of another package to the customer. An example might be a travel agent selling a weekend theatre break in London. You need to have sight of all ads that are used by third parties to ensure that your business is promoted in the image and style that you want.

8 Size of print. Any print material that you produce must be easy to read. The more difficult it is to read, the less likely it is that it will be read and therefore the money spent producing it will be wasted. A key factor is the size of print used. The most common print type is 9 point; anything smaller is not recommended. You should never reduce the size of print beyond this just to get more words on the page. Instead, have another look at the copy and edit it.

9 Reversed colours. You will have seen print material that looks as though white has been printed on black. In fact, it is black printing with spaces left for the white, in other words the print colours are reversed. Market research has shown that this style is more difficult to read, so avoid using it.

10 White space sells. Imagine paper with nothing written on it. The idea of it selling more sounds impossible. However, the right amount and location of white space will make your message easier to read. A wide margin at the left-hand edge assists the eye to focus on each line. Also, rather than large blocks of print you may want to double space the lines, or have the headlines with more space around them to make them stand out.

11 Gain and maintain interest. When you have large amounts of copy it can be very off-putting and the reader never gets started. To overcome this, enlarge and drop the first letter of the first word. The top of the letter remains in line with the other letters but it drops below the bottom of the line on to the next or several lines. This can often be seen in magazine articles because it attracts the eye to the start of the piece.

   To maintain interest you can break up the print using cross-heads (subheadings). These are short headlines that summarize the contents of the next few paragraphs. This technique has been used in this book because it tells readers what is coming and encourages them to read on.

12 Caption pictures. Too often a reader will see superb photographs but have no idea what they refer to. Use a caption, that is a few words that describe the relevance of the picture, e.g. 'The view from the honeymoon suite', 'The superb new salad bar'.

13 Give it 'you' appeal. There is a great tendency to talk about what 'we' have to offer: 'We provide a warm

welcome'; 'We serve fresh food'; 'We give a free lollipop to each child'. These words can be improved with 'You' appeal, for example: 'You will receive a warm welcome'; 'You will enjoy the selection of freshly prepared food'; 'Your child will receive a free lollipop'.

The same applies when writing letters to customers. Do not use 'I' because the hospitality industry is about caring for 'You', the customer.

14 The right-hand page. When you pick up your local paper, consider what you do, and which pages you look at first. The majority of people look at right-hand pages first, that is the odd-numbered ones. They also look at the corners first. So, if you have a choice of where the ad appears on a page then consider these points for maximum impact and readership.

## Summary

1 There are many reasons why businesses advertise.
2 You control what goes into the ad, but the customer's view is subjective.
3 Advertising is made up of three groups. You, the advertiser; the agencies or creators; the media.
4 Promotional objectives are set that support the overall business objectives.
5 The advertising brief informs others about what you want to achieve.
6 Visualize your target audience.
7 Attention, Interest, Desire and Action are what a good ad achieves.
8 There are four key functions in an advertising agency.
9 There is a variety of media you can use; they all have strengths and weaknesses.
10 There are no rules of advertising but the results of market research, experience and the workings of the human eye help.

## Key questions

1 What do you want to advertise?
2 What do you want to achieve?
3 How would you visualize your target audience?
4 Which is better for you – an agency or do-it-yourself, and why?
5 What ads gain your attention and interest, and why?
6 Which medium will be best for your needs?
7 How can your recent ads be improved?

# 10
# Public relations

Public relations, or PR as it is usually known, is a very misunderstood subject. Too often it is seen as a cheap form of advertising, or a way of getting a mention for the chairman. This situation is further complicated as many people have a fear about talking to the media. This fear is sometimes based on a painful past experience by a colleague or a friend which resulted in bad publicity. PR should be seen as a very useful tool which is effective and very good value for money.

## What is PR?

The Institute of Public Relations describes it as follows:

> Public relations practice is the planned and sustained effort to establish and maintain goodwill and mutual understanding between an organisation and its publics.

This definition splits into four key areas:

1 *Planning*. Like all aspects of marketing it has to be planned, or your PR activity will be haphazard and disjointed. As with all aspects of the promotional mix you need to set the objectives at the start.

2 *Sustained activity*. You cannot achieve the objectives of PR, such as understanding and goodwill, unless your activity is sustained. It is pointless having two articles in your local

paper in December if you are not featured again until the following August. PR is a week-in, week-out activity.

3 *Understanding and goodwill.* The purpose of PR is to create understanding and goodwill. To create understanding you need to give customers knowledge, because from knowledge comes understanding, and from understanding comes goodwill.

4 *Publics.* In the previous chapter on advertising we looked at the target audience for the ad. Your PR activity should also be directed at key groups which, in PR terms, are known as 'publics'. They are people such as employees, potential employees, local opinion formers, the local community, etc.

## Setting the PR objective

As with advertising, the promotional objective for PR will fit in with the overall business objective. They must also complement the other promotional objectives that you set for each of the promotional tools you are using. I believe it helpful to give more detail to the PR objective. You should include the media to be used, the timing of the campaign, the target publics and the activity. Let us look at how our case studies might express their PR objectives.

### The hotel

To create awareness of the wedding package offered by the hotel with 40 per cent of 20–35 year olds within a 20-mile radius. This will be achieved by sending details of all couples who have receptions at the hotel to the local paper and by presenting the couple with their own specially engraved cake-knife from the hotel. This offer would last one year.

## The restaurant

To provide a free minibus from the exhibition centre to the restaurant after conference finish for delegates and exhibitors to enjoy a 'Happy Hour' with free transport back to their hotels afterwards. To be promoted using a flyer inserted into the conference pack at the six largest conferences in the next eight months.

## The pub

To separate the pub from others within the town by showing its caring nature to the local community. To be achieved by raising £500 for new toys at the children's ward of the local hospital within three months, with the fund-raising events being featured in the local free newspaper.

## The fast-food restaurant

To sponsor three new litter bins in the high street, via the local authority, to create understanding among shoppers about the restaurant's concern for litter in the high street.

## The staff restaurant

To demonstrate to employees the healthiness of the food available in the new salad bar during the first month of operation, by inviting in a group of local doctors to taste the food. The event to be featured in the company's newsletter.

The expansion of the PR objective in this way clarifies what you want to achieve. It will keep your activity well focused on the chosen media and ensure that you are talking to the targeted publics.

## What are 'publics'?

We have already said that 'publics' is a PR term that is similar to the term 'target audience' in advertising. The publics for the hospitality industry can be generalized and put into the following categories.

1  the local community,
2  potential employees,
3  existing employees,
4  suppliers,
5  customers,
6  opinion formers.

*The local community*: this consists of your business neighbours and the people who live in your local area. They are the people complaining to the fast-food restaurant manager about the litter outside the restaurant and the reason he has decided to sponsor the litter bins. You always need good PR with this public because it will contain so many existing and potential customers.

*Potential employees*: many companies have put considerable resources into this area as they have been concerned about the decline in the number of school leavers. However, as this book is being written unemployment is rising, with many jobs being shed from this industry and many others. Therefore the available labour market is expanding. This will mean that many future employees will come from other industries. If this situation happened to our hotelier, how could he use it for PR purposes? He employed a new hall porter who had previously worked in a local factory for 20 years before being made redundant. The hotelier took him on, trained him, encouraged him and after nine months he was promoted to head porter. The manager contacted the local paper and they did a feature about the porter and how he had been trained in his new job. When he next advertised a vacancy in reception he found that many more local people were interested, with applications from people in local offices and banks.

*Existing employees*: this public is vital to any service industry; these are the people responsible for delivering the service to customers. But how much attention do you give them? Are they kept well informed about what is going on in your business? Do you regularly listen to their ideas and encourage their input? If not, then how can they promote and sell your business to others?

*Suppliers*: they can be both local and national, and cover a whole range of products from food to cleaning materials. They must not be forgotten because you may well need their help for a sales promotion, sponsorship and, in the case of the bank manager, for continuing in business.

*Customers*: you may have already identified the various types of customer, using the customer/service matrix. However, one group is often forgotten, and that is children. Children have considerable influence over parents' choice, and PR can be a great help. A visit by Santa, a free lollipop at the end of a meal, special children's parties are all aimed at creating goodwill with children and their parents.

*Opinion formers*: this public is much wider than you might first consider. It is not linked just to local and national politicians but includes teachers, doctors, clergy, professional bodies in the industry, local organizations such as Rotary and Tourist Boards. Our case studies targeted opinion formers. The staff restaurant invited in local doctors and the fast-food restaurant worked with the local authority on the litter bins. The last opinion former, but perhaps the most important, is the past customer. They can influence many future purchase decisions just by what they say about your business to friends and business colleagues.

## The media for PR

In the chapter on advertising we looked at the various types of media that were available. Most of them are suitable for PR activity, however there are some new ones that are specific to PR. What are they, and how could they be used by our case studies?

*Audio visual presentations*: these could use OHPs (overhead projectors), flip-charts, or slides. Our hotelier produced a slide-show about the hotel and how he proposed to improve it over the next few years. He wrote to all the local organizations such as the WI, Round Table, etc., and he presented it to them at their various meetings.

*Videos*: to produce an individual video for your business could be too expensive but you may be able to adapt the use of an existing one. For example, our hotelier was approached by a conference organizer from another part of the country. They wanted to know what could be organized for the wives of delegates attending a clients' conference. The hotelier discovered a video promoting the area produced by the local tourist board and sent it off to them. You may say that this was a selling activity; I believe that it created understanding and goodwill and was therefore a PR activity.

*Notice boards*: these are too often dull and boring because they only contain documents that are legal requirements. Notice boards are a great way of keeping employees informed about what is happening in your business. Our restaurateur produced a monthly graph which showed the number of conference packages sold each month against the target. If they beat the target he offered all the staff a free drink, at a convenient time, and said thank you for all their efforts.

*House newspapers*: there has been a tremendous growth in this area, with many more large companies seeing the benefit of good communications with staff. Our staff restaurant manageress could use this media to run a series of stories about healthy eating and what is now available at lunchtime. She decided to run competitions with chances of winning meals at lunchtime and special hampers at Christmas. Some companies have made their house newspapers into audio tapes so that staff can listen to them in their car and at work.

*Exhibitions*: our restaurateur could take stand space at the various exhibitions that are being held in support of the various conferences. This would give him the chance to contact delegates and other stand holders. He could ask people to place their business cards in a drum with a chance to win a champagne dinner for two. From the business cards he would be able to create a mailing list.

*Recruitment literature*: during their academic careers students start to look at their future career opportunities. Many companies now invest considerable sums in the production of suitable literature. This was well beyond the means of our hotelier. He decided to make contact with the careers master of the local school and invited a group of pupils to go round the hotel. The manager arranged a special cookery demonstration by the head chef. He then talked about the various career opportunities available in the industry and how he had reached his current position. This created goodwill among the publics of the teaching staff, the children and their parents.

*Educational literature*: as with recruitment, some companies have sponsored teachers' packs for schools or provided prizes for local colleges. Our fast-food restaurant manager decided to do a project with a local primary school as part of a school and industry initiative. This is where children do a project about a local business and learn how it operates. You can find out more from your local education authority.

## Setting the PR budget

A major difference between PR and advertising is that you do not buy PR space. This does not mean that you do not have costs. There are obvious costs when you agree a sponsorship or employ a PR agency. However, there are still costs if you decide to do it yourself – such as staff time, postage, telephone calls, stationery, expenses and entertaining. They should be identified and controlled.

We have already said that PR must be planned. However, some PR opportunities can arise at very short notice. Your budget should contain a contingency element so that you can respond quickly to this event. For example, our publican was raising money for new toys at the hospital when he discovered that a local disabled child's home had been burgled and her new computer stolen. He immediately organized a special event to raise money and was able to replace the computer within a few weeks.

One of the major factors in setting the budget is whether to use an agency or to do it yourself.

## PR: in-house or agency?

You will need to consider the advantages and disadvantages of each option. There is no right or wrong answer, every business will have different requirements or level of skills in-house.

The advantages of using an agency:

● Their advice is likely to be more objective.
● They will have a wider and greater depth of experience.
● Their contacts with the media, printers, photographers and other suppliers will be better.

The disadvantages of using an agency:

● It can never be a full service because you are only buying a number of hours.
● They will have a number of clients and therefore you share their resources according to the amount of your fee and its relationship to the size of the agency.
● They are less likely to have an intimate knowledge of your industry.
● Some consultancies have a number of junior and therefore less experienced staff who may be deputed to be your main contact.

The advantages of do-it-yourself:

● You are working solely for the one client.
● You have an intimate knowledge of your business and the industry.
● It is cheaper.
● Communications will be simpler due to better access of information within the company.

The disadvantages of do-it-yourself:

● The advice will not be independent and could be biased.
● It will take time to build up contacts with the media.
● Your business may not be close to the centres of the media.
● Inexperience and lack of knowledge of the person carrying out the PR activity.

One often finds that the smaller the business, the more likely you are to use a PR consultant. The larger the company, the more likely you are to have your own in-house team.

## The press release

The single most important PR tool is the press release because it is the link between you and the media. However, the first step is to create a list of all the media that you may want to approach. This may include local TV and radio, national, regional and local newspapers, industry magazines, etc. You will not send every press release to every medium because the story may not be appropriate.

For example, our fast-food restaurant may send out a story to the local newspaper about sponsoring the local refuse bins but this would not be of interest to the catering magazines.

The appropriate media for each press release are identified from the master list that you have created. The master list can be prepared from the information the local library will have in the reference section. Alternatively, you can buy a copy of *The Writers Handbook* (published by Macmillan), which is updated each year.

### Writing a press release

There is one drawback to the success of your press release, and that is the sheer number of them that arrive on the editor's desk. An editor can receive hundreds every day but is only likely to use 20 per cent. You must make sure that your press release stands out from the others. This is easier said than done but the following advice will be helpful.

1  You must make editors' lives easier. They only have a few seconds to decide which story to cover. You only get one chance to make an impression. The first few words are vital, so you should spend the most amount of time on the headline and the first paragraph.

   These should attract the editor's interest and include the subject matter and the gist of the story. The remaining paragraphs are there to support the information contained within that first paragraph.

2  Write the release with the intention that it can be printed as written. The fewer alterations that have to be made by the editor, the greater the chance of it being printed.

3  Head the page with the words 'PRESS RELEASE'. This could be with specially printed notepaper or you can buy a rubber stamp for under £10. The reason is to ensure that it stands out from other mail.

4  We looked at the width of margins in the chapter on advertising. The same applies here, however a wide margin also gives an editor space to make alterations or comments for the printer or journalist covering the story.

5  Use a serif typeface that the editor is used to reading. Look at the targeted media to see which typefaces are most commonly used.

6  Double space the lines of type. This gives extra space for the editor to make notes.

7  Do not use cross-headings (subheadings within the body of the text) unless it is a very long piece of copy because they would not be used by the paper.

8 Capital letters should only be used for names of individuals, organizations and places.

9 Use quotation marks for quoted speech only and not to emphasize a point. Quotes give a press release life provided they are not full of clichés and fit in with the storyline. Always make sure that you attribute a name and position to the quote, e.g. 'Mr David Smith, Catering Manager, said . . . '

10 Do not underline. You never see this used in the papers and it will only mean that the editor has to make a correction.

11 Do not indent the first paragraph for the same reason that we identified in point 10.

12 When you are using numbers spell out one to nine. After that use figures unless it is a very large number or cash.

13 If you are using abbreviations make sure you do not use full points between them, for example BBC not B.B.C.

14 If you are continuing from the front page to a second page then clearly state that the story is continued, otherwise the editor may stop reading.

15 Write dates as 'January 1' and not 'January 1st'.

16 If you are sending in photographs then they should be 10 inches by 8 inches, black and white glossy, with captions written on the back and the names of all the people shown, left to right.

17 Provide a name and a telephone number for the person to contact for further information at the bottom of the final sheet.

## Assessing the results

The main reason for setting an objective at the start is so that we can measure the results. PR can be measured in three ways:

1  using research,
2  from feedback,
3  by observation.

If we look at our case studies then we can see how each of the above methods is used.

### The hotel

Our hotelier had a detailed objective about creating awareness among 40 per cent of a specific age group. The success of this campaign could be analysed by market research to find out if the relevant age group were aware of the wedding package that was available.

### The pub

The publican, who was raising money for the local hospital, could judge his success on the feedback that he receives. It might be in the form of thank you or congratulatory letters, comments from customers, press cuttings or radio broadcasts.

### The staff restaurant

Our staff restaurant manageress could establish the success of the new salad bar by observing what customers chose, by analysing till receipts, and by being aware of how many new faces came into the restaurant.

PR is a vital part of the marketing mix because, to misquote a well-known lager advertisement. 'It reaches the parts advertising fails to reach'. However, you must remember to persevere even if your last three press releases have not been used. There are times when the competition for stories in the media is intense and there are other times when the media is struggling to fill the pages. So keep on sending out the press releases but remember the points we discussed earlier in this chapter.

## Summary

1 PR is the planned and sustained effort to establish and maintain goodwill and mutual understanding between an organization and its publics.
2 Set a PR objective that includes the media, the time-span, the publics and activity.
3 'Publics' is a PR term that means the target audience. It includes the local community, potential and existing employees, suppliers, customers and opinion formers.
4 There are new types of media that you can consider such as audio visual aids, exhibitions, educational and recruitment literature.
5 You need to consider the advantages and disadvantages of employing an agency or doing it yourself.
6 Editors receive hundreds of press releases every day; ensure that the first paragraph attracts their attention.
7 PR can be assessed by using research, feedback and observation.

## Key questions

1 Is your PR sustained? If not, how can you change the situation?
2 Who are your key PR publics?
3 What are your PR objectives?
4 Which media will be best to achieve your objectives?
5 How can you improve your press releases?
6 Which method of PR assessment will you use?

# 11
# Sales promotion

Over the last few years we have seen a dramatic increase in the number of sales promotions being used by companies of all sizes. It is not a question of just reducing price and printing some promotional literature – so what is it?

## What is sales promotion?

The Institute of Sales Promotion defines it as follows:

> Sales promotion comprises that range of techniques used to attain sales/marketing objectives in a cost effective manner by adding value to a product or service either to intermediaries or end-users, normally but not exclusively within a defined time period.

This clearly identifies the importance of adding value. We have already looked at the importance of customer benefits that separate one product from another. Sales promotion takes this differentiation to another level by adding value with the aim of completing a sale.

Customers buy more often when they feel they are getting good value for money. When you add extra value you are improving customer perceptions of the product or service. As we will see in this chapter it can be done in a variety of ways. The greater the value, the more likely you are to achieve the sales objective set.

## Setting the objectives

Customers may consider buying a whole range of your hospitality products or those offered by your competitors. Sales promotion focuses their attention on one of them at a time and provides the incentive to buy.

The sales promotion could fit into any one of the following general objectives:

- increasing the volume of sales,
- obtaining new customers,
- encouraging repeat purchase,
- increasing the range of products bought by existing customers,
- creating interest and awareness of new or improved products,
- moving customers' concerns away from the price being offered.

As with all the promotional tools your sales promotion objectives will fit into the overall business objectives. You need to define the problem you want to overcome so that your objective is clear.

Let us look again at our case studies and identify some objectives for them.

### The hotel

To lengthen the summer wedding season into March and October by offering one free wedding package for every 10 booked. To sell six weddings with an average of 100 covers in these months next year.

### The restaurant

To generate repeat custom from the weekend family lunch market by offering three Sunday lunches for the price of two for any party of four or more during the months of January, February and March (excluding Mother's Day). To achieve an increase of 10 per cent extra customers over last year.

### The pub

The publican aimed to increase the sale of liqueurs by 15 per cent during the month of December at Christmas parties. Every time a measure of a particular brandy was sold the brandy supplier donated 5p towards the children's ward charity.

### The fast-food restaurant

After the first three months of the home delivery service they wanted to sell an average of 250 side salads extra per week. All customers who ordered one of the range of salads qualified for a competition to win a trip to the new Disney Theme Park outside Paris.

### The staff restaurant

They wanted to create interest and awareness of the new salad bar among non-users of the restaurant. They offered a £1 voucher off a salad bar meal in the company newspaper to be taken on a Monday or Friday (the quietest days) in the next six weeks.

## Why use sales promotion?

Sales promotions have a number of benefits:

1 They work.
2 They are put on for a specific time.
3 They are easy to monitor. You can measure the effect on sales on a daily basis against the target set.

4 They are fun to do and create interest among staff and customers.
5 They can be set up quickly and can help to solve short-term sales decline.
6 It is easier to direct them at a specific target audience, for example, our restaurateur and the family lunch market.

## Using sales promotion tactically or strategically

Sales promotions' initial main aim was to solve a short-term decline in sales and profitability. Many companies have a number of different promotional concepts that they can put into operation at very short notice.

You identify the problem, establish a sales promotion and monitor the results. This is the tactical approach and the one that ignores the full potential of sales promotion.

If you adopt a long-term or strategic approach with a series of different sales promotions over a period of time it will bring you extra benefits.

1 Your promotions can be built together to achieve continuity.
2 This will save you both time and money.
3 It is easier to promote the same image over a series of promotions rather than one-offs.
4 When sales promotion is fully incorporated into the marketing plan it enables the customer benefits to be fully promoted through all the promotional tools.

The strategic use of sales promotion will be differently applied in each of our case studies. For example, the hotelier could have a whole series of food and beverage sales promotions that run in different parts of the hotel from one week to another. It may be a 'Spanish Food' event in the restaurant followed by a 'Summer Fruits' in the bar and then a 'Two for the price of one' night in hotel accommodation.

Our staff restaurant could not adopt this approach because it is a single outlet. If they had a sales promotion every week it would become the norm and the possibility of generating interest would disappear. Instead they could hold regular two-weekly promotions and as one ends they start to create awareness of the next promotion.

## Planning a sales promotion

Before we look at the various types of sales promotion, let us clarify the questions that you need to answer at the outset.

1  What business sales problem do you want to solve?
2  What is your promotional objective?
3  Who is the target audience?
4  How much are you able to spend on the promotion?
5  What factors will limit the promotion? This might be timing, the size of the premises, what your competitors are doing, etc.
6  How will the results be evaluated?

## What types of sales promotion are available?

Sales promotions fall into a number of categories. Within each category there are a whole number of ideas that can be developed. Let us look at the categories and see how our case studies could use them.

1  *Immediate price offer*: this is where a discount is offered against a declared price at the time of purchase.
   (a)  Our hotelier offers a price discount for any conference organizer that books more than 10 rooms between October and March.
   (b)  The restaurant gives a seasonal reduction off restaurant meals during January and February because these months are normally quiet.

(c) The publican offers a 5 per cent discount for all function bills that are paid on the night because of the benefit it brings to his cash flow.

(d) The fast-food restaurant offers 50 p off every pizza ordered on a Monday.

(e) The staff restaurant offers a special introductory offer for the new salad bar on the first three days of opening.

2 *Delayed price offer*; this is where a discount is offered against a declared price but is not immediately available at the time of purchase.

(a) An overriding discount is offered to certain companies that use the hotel on a regular basis for conferences. An income figure is set at the start of the year between the hotel and the companies concerned. If the companies spend more they get an extra 2 per cent discount.

(b) Our restaurateur gave a third meal free if the customers came for two family meals for four or more within three months.

(c) The staff restaurant gave out future purchase coupons on a Wednesday, which was the busiest day of the week. Customers could redeem them on any Monday or Friday the following week, those being the quietest days.

3 *Immediate free offer*: this provides a premium to the customer for purchasing a particular product. A premium is an extra benefit which comes in the form of a piece of merchandise. It is not a question of reducing price but adding value with extra products.

(a) Our hotel offered two nights for the price of one at certain times of the year.

(b) The fast-food restaurant gave customers a medium size cola if they ordered a burger after 2 p.m.

(c) The publican sold doubles for the price of a single for the first hour of opening between Monday and Thursday evenings.

4 *Delayed free offer*: this is where customers collect a number of qualifying proofs of purchase and then send them in to collect their offer. It encourages repeat purchases at the same establishment and thus increases loyalty to the same product or service.

(a) Our hotelier introduced a scheme whereby every guest who stayed at the hotel was given a token each time they stayed there. When guests had collected five they could exchange them for six bottles of wine. Alternatively, they could save up 10 and qualify for a free night's accommodation and dinner for two on a Saturday night.

(b) The publican had a similar system with a card being stamped when people purchased a new brand of lager. The first stamp was given away free and when they had reached 10 they could have a free pint.

5 *Self-liquidating promotions*: this is where the customer or supplier pays for all the costs of the premium gift. So, if the gift is a golf umbrella and it costs £4.00 plus postage and packing then this is what the customer pays, but the customer benefits because you have bought at trade price and are adding no margin. This type of promotion could well be organized by your suppliers for you to take advantage of.

(a) The manufacturer of crisps that were supplied to the pub offered customers the chance to purchase a special teddy bear if they sent off three crisp packets plus £2.99.

(b) The staff restaurant introduced frozen yoghurt and the supplier paid for a promotion to increase awareness of the product. At the end of the promotion sales had reached a sufficient level to pay for all the costs involved, which meant it had been self-liquidating.

6 *Prize promotions*: these offer the chance to win something and have two advantages:

(a) The cost can be more easily controlled because you are not dependent on the number of people taking up the offer. In other promotions the offer is open to every purchaser.

(b) The prize offered can be much larger.

However, the drawback is that the customers are not guaranteed the added value with every item purchased; they only have a *chance* of getting it. There are four types of prize promotion:

- competitions,
- games,
- draws,
- lotteries.

A word of warning about these types of promotion. There are a number of legal requirements that can affect the style of the promotion. It is therefore advisable to gain professional help from a sales promotion company or other source. We will come back to this point.

A competition requires customers to use their skill and judgement when they have made a purchase. Our catering manager could give an entry form to everyone buying a meal at lunchtime. The competition could ask them to use their skill and judgement to choose a balanced menu for a dinner party from a selection of dishes. A tie-breaker could be introduced to come up with a final winner, e.g. 'I prefer to select a healthy meal option because .................. (please complete in not more than 20 words).'

Promotional games require no skill and they incorporate a predetermined chance to win. However, they would have to be given to anyone who asked, as no proof of purchase is required. For example, our fast-food restaurant gave out a scratch-card game to every customer. If they scratched off the appropriate symbols then they could win free portions of chips or drinks. However, each card must have a chance of winning.

Draws offer a single or number of prizes that can be won by the chance selection of one or more tickets. Our hotelier could offer a bottle of champagne as a prize for those guests who leave their business card in a top hat. (Giving him the opportunity to compile a mailing list from the names and addresses.)

A lottery is similar to a draw but you have to pay to enter. It is strictly controlled by the Lotteries and Amusements Act 1976 and it is unlikely that you would use it.

7 *A charitable promotion*: there are two ways this could work.

(a) An event. This could be a dinner and dance or a boxing evening but whatever it is you would make the profit from the event. In order to help the charity you would organize a tombola or auction. This type of function is very different from the PR charity event where our hotelier donated the use of his ballroom so that the charity could organize a tea dance to raise money.

(b) Collections. This is most likely to be organized by one of your suppliers as an on-pack offer. The supplier agrees to pay a specific amount to a charity, for example for every packet of nuts that is sold by the publican, the company will donate 5p, up to a maximum of £10,000.

## The law relating to sales promotion

There is not only law that affects sales promotion there is also a code of practice which is controlled by the Advertising Standards Authority. In simple terms, sales promotions have, like advertising, to be legal, decent, honest and truthful. If you are creating your own promotion and want to make sure it complies with the code, then a free and quick service is available to you. It is run by:

The Code of Advertising Practice Committee
2–16 Torrington Place
London WC1E 7HN
Telephone: 071 580 5555

They also provide a free booklet entitled: *The British Code of Sales Promotion Practice*. This provides details of the scope of the code, definitions, the basic principles and general guidelines.

If you are still in doubt then it is advisable to get a solicitor's advice.

## Evaluating the results

This process is easier than with some of the other promotional tools providing that the objective that you gave set either specific sales targets, percentage increases or profit forecasts. These can all be measured precisely from your analysis of sales and income.

It is not just a question of how many customers took up the offer. For example, our restaurateur introduced a summer sales promotion that offered two meals for the price of one if customers came in between 6 p.m. and 7.30 p.m. Even though only 50 customers took up the offer it brought in a total of 250 customers during the appropriate time-span. Sales were up 10 per cent on forecast. If he had looked just at the take-up he could have deemed it a failure.

## Summary

1 Sales promotion adds value to the product or service.
2 It was originally created to overcome short-term sales decline.
3 However, it can have both a strategic and tactical use.
4 There is a variety of different sales promotion techniques such as immediate and delayed price offers, free offers, self-liquidating promotions, prize competitions.
5 There is a voluntary code of practice which is controlled by the Advertising Standards Authority. They offer a free service to check that your promotion complies with the code.

## Key questions

1  What sales problems do you need to rectify?
2  What are your sales promotion objectives?
3  How can you add value to your products and services?
4  What type of promotion will suit your needs?
5  How will you ensure that the promotion complies with the code of practice?

# 12
## An introduction to personal selling

You will have heard some people described as 'born sales-people' or having 'real salesmanship'. But what does this mean?

A salesperson has been described as a person who can stand more rejection than anyone else. This may be an over-exaggeration, however it does highlight the most important requirement for selling. You must be in a positive frame of mind and then you must retain it even if each potential customer you meet decides against purchasing from you.

Look at every customer and potential customer as a new challenge because they have nothing to do with the person you spoke to yesterday, or an hour ago. They may have business to give you, but you will never find out until you talk to them.

The dictionary describes salesmanship as 'the skill in finding customers'. As we will see later in this chapter, you already have an enormous amount of information about customers. It is now a question of using it effectively.

### But why sell?

Selling may be a novel experience for you. Someone else may have been given the responsibility for selling and you may not like the idea of having to do it. However, everyone has the ability to sell and everyone, including you, must be actively selling.

The reasons for this are simple:

1 Very little happens in your business until a sale is made. The chef may be busy preparing food but your business does not really start until a customer wants to buy.
2 Sales bring in income, income pays your wages. No income, no jobs or wages.
3 Increased sales bring in increased profits which provide job security.

## There are many opportunities to sell

Everyone has a sales responsibility. You may be talking to someone in the lounge and asking 'Would you like some biscuits with your coffee?' Alternatively, it could be selling an extra course to a function organizer. The opportunities to sell are endless and cannot all be included in this chapter.

What we have done is to introduce you to the concepts of personal selling. This chapter looks at identifying potential customers to create a sales database, then looks at gaining the appointment with the potential customer and how to get the best results out of that appointment. Many of the techniques described can be used for other selling situations, for example asking questions and closing the sale. We have also included some helpful hints which, hopefully, will help you avoid some of the more common pitfalls. But let us start by defining what we mean by selling.

## What is selling?

Selling is about converting interest in a product into a decision to purchase. A great deal of effort goes into the creation of interest, such as advertising, PR and direct mail. The selling process is about turning that interest into actual cash in the tills, either immediately or at some time in the future.

Sales activity does not have to create an immediate sale. In fact research suggests that it takes five contacts to make one sale. In those five contacts you may need to:

1 Create awareness of you and your business.
2 Establish rapport with the potential customer.
3 Understand the customer needs.
4 Provide more information.
5 Sell the benefits of what you have to offer.
6 Close the sale.

The process does not end there. You will then provide the service and at this point you may want to create awareness of other services and so the process continues.

## Setting the objective

You will now realize that this is the first stage for any of the promotional tools and the sales objective must fit in with the overall business objectives that have already been set.

However, your sales objective will change as you progress through the selling process. For example, it could be expressed as:

1 To increase total sales by 10 per cent in the next financial year.
2 To increase total sales by £20,000 in the six winter months.
3 To increase room occupancy from 60 per cent to 65 per cent in October and November.
4 To increase average spend for a week-day bar snack lunch from £3.00 to £4.00 over the next three months.
5 To increase the number of restaurant covers served from an average of 600 per week to 665 in the four-week run-up to Christmas.

This second set of objectives is not only quantifiable but also has a specific time-span.

But how could these different types of sales objectives be applied to our case studies and our hotelier in particular?

## *The hotel*

Our hotelier wants to expand his residential conference business over the next 12 months. He sets himself the following overall sales objective: to sell an extra 1200 bed nights in the financial year 1992–93 on the all inclusive conference rate of £75.00.

However to achieve this he needs to set a number of supporting objectives to ensure that the overall objective can be achieved. For example:

1 To establish the names and addresses of the top 100 companies that buy conference space within a 30-mile radius of the hotel.
2 To place them in priority order as far as number of potential bed nights are concerned.
3 To establish the name and title of the person responsible for making the booking.
4 To gain an appointment to see 20 of the top 25 contacts in the first three months and 80 of the top 100 by the end of the financial year.
5 To establish the conference needs and requirements of those 20 contacts visited in the first three months and the 80 by the end of the financial year.
6 To identify potential sales of 10 000 bed nights over the next two years among the 80 contacts made.
7 To obtain confirmed bookings of 1000 conference bed nights in the first six months.

You will now see that from an overall objective, a series of other sales objectives must fit in. So, if we set overall objectives for the other case studies, ask yourself what other objectives should they set?

## *The restaurant*

To sell 400 conference dinner packages over the next six months.

### The pub

To increase the number of Christmas parties in the month of December from 50 to 70.

### The staff restaurant

To sell one extra function per month, with a sales value of £750 in the next 12 months.

Having set the objective there is one vital management skill that you must develop to achieve success. It is creating and maintaining a positive attitude.

## Positive attitudes

How often do you feel below par, tired or fed up? We all do at some time or another. The secret is never to let customers or staff know when this is.

If you become negative it will not be long before your assistant is negative and then your staff. Once staff are negative the standards of service decline, customers get upset and are less likely to use your services again.

You will gain enormous benefit if you can create a permanent positive attitude. Everyone around you will become positive, which will mean problems are quickly solved and the standards of service maintained.

When you are making personal sales calls the attitude you put across is even more important. It may sound easy, but imagine you have visited six potential clients in a day and not obtained a single sale. You feel fed up and this attitude is put across to the next potential client who will pick up the 'negative vibes' and is unlikely to be put into a buying mood.

You never know on which personal sales call you will make a sale. You must always believe that your next sales call is the one that will generate £10,000 of business. So remain positive at all times and ensure that the positive attitudes are maintained and continued in all parts of your life.

## Creating the sales database

Before you carry out a personal sales call you need to identify potential customers. This could be done in a variety of ways:

1 By desk research.
2 By using trade and local directories.
3 From information within your business, such as past customer records; these could be registration cards, or the banqueting and restaurant diaries.
4 From a previous sales database – it is surprising how often one finds an old one that has not been used for some time.
5 From debtors lists – many of your past customers will have had credit, and their accounts will be in your debtor records, but are they still using your business and, if not, why not?
6 From the local papers – these have a whole host of background information such as new businesses opening, new appointments, job vacancies, etc.

This information then needs to be collated and made into a sales database. The information you need for each potential customer is:

1 Full name.
2 Title.
3 Company name.
4 Full address.
5 Telephone number.
6 Type of business they are in.
7 Type of product or service they have used in the past.
8 Space for further information, e.g. date when contacted, points discussed, further action, etc.

| Jan | Feb | Mar | Apl | May | Jun | Jul | Aug | Sep | Oct | Nov | Dec |
|-----|-----|-----|-----|-----|-----|-----|-----|-----|-----|-----|-----|

| Organization: | | | Type: | | Code: |
|---|---|---|---|---|---|

Address:

| | Phone Nos: | Telex: |
|---|---|---|

| Contact: | Contact: |
|---|---|
| Position: | Position: |
| Contact: | Contact: |
| Position: | Position: |

Source:

| Date contacted | Items discussed | Action to be taken |
|----------------|-----------------|--------------------|
| | | |
| | | |
| | | |
| | | |
| | | |
| | | |
| | | |
| | | |
| | | |
| | | |
| | | |
| | | |
| | | |
| | | |
| | | |
| | | |
| | | |
| | | |
| | | |
| | | |

**Figure 12.1**

An example of a page from a sales database can be seen in Figure 12.1.

You will find gaps in the information. These can be quickly filled by making a telephone call and asking the telephonist of the appropriate company for the information.

One extra piece of information that is very useful is the name of your contact's secretary. If your contact is not in the office you will find it much easier to talk to the secretary by name.

You will need to create one sheet for each potential customer and place them in an appropriate file in alphabetical order. You now have a sales database to work from.

## Making the appointment

This may be done over the telephone. However, you must first plan your call and consider what you are going to say. I used the approach that follows; it helped me increase my success rate in gaining appointments because it overcame many of the objections.

1  Ensure that you have all the details as described above, including the first name of the secretary.
2  Make sure that you cannot be disturbed and that you are in a positive frame of mind.
3  Telephone the company and ask for the contact. You will usually be put through to the secretary; use his or her first name.
4  Ask to speak to the boss using both his/her first and surname.
5  When the secretary asks you what it is about ignore the question and say 'it really was John Smith that I wanted to speak to'. Many people will put you through at this stage.
6  If the boss is not there then find out when it will be convenient to phone back, and ensure you do so at the stated time.
7  When you are put through to your contact, you will need to have prepared a script of what you want to say. This will

cover who you are, why you want to see him/her and the benefits that could accrue as a result. Be prepared for objections, so devise answers to overcome them.

8 During the conversation ask for an appointment and offer two or three alternative dates. This makes it more difficult to turn them all down.

9 When you have an appointment confirm it in writing.

This approach works but it does take practice to carry it off with confidence.

However, you may prefer to write to your contact first. In the letter you would use the points that you had prepared for your telephone script. Then the last paragraph you could write:

'Please may I come and discuss these points with you? I will telephone your secretary next week to make an appointment, and I look forward to seeing you in the near future.'

When you phone the secretary to make your appointment refer to your letter.

## The sales appointment

You have now obtained your appointment and confirmed the time and date. The next stage is to understand the various processes of the sales call. They are:

1 set an objective for the call,
2 establish rapport,
3 ask questions,
4 sell benefits not features,
5 ask for the order,
6 close the sale,
7 shut up and get out.

### Set an objective for the call

Before you make your personal sales call, write down what you want to get out of it. The purpose is not always going to be to make a sale. It could be to find out more about the client to see if, and how often, they use hotels. The purpose of setting this objective is to ensure that you can establish whether or not you were successful.

## Establish rapport

People buy people. Buyers buy because they trust and believe the people they are buying from. So you need to establish a rapport with the potential buyer. This may take time to develop, but one important point is to listen to what you are told. It sounds simple, but too often the salesperson does not listen and only hears what they want to hear.

## Ask questions

You need to ask questions for a number of reasons:

1 to establish rapport,
2 to obtain information,
3 to clarify points of information,
4 to close a sale, e.g. 'When would you like the booking for?'

There are two basic types of questions. The first are closed questions that will give you the answers Yes and No. They are used for clarifying points, e.g. 'Did you want a room with bath?'

The second type are open questions and they are used to gain more information from the potential customer, e.g. 'How often do you use hotels?' Open questions normally start with one of the following words: 'how', 'what', 'why', 'when', 'where', 'who'. We all tend to ask closed questions and you will need to practise the technique of asking open questions.

When you are asking questions keep probing for more information. For example, if you ask 'when do you use hotels?' and the answer is 'very rarely', ask who else in the company will use hotels. In this situation you may find out that you are talking to the wrong person.

Ask questions and keep asking them so that you can find out as much information as possible.

## Sell benefits not features

We looked at this in the chapter on advertising. In the personal sales call it is even more important to sell the right benefits to the right customer. The more information you have gathered by questioning, the easier the process is.

A feature is a physical attribute of your business, e.g. a room with a private bathroom. You need to be aware of all your features and then turn them into benefits. This can be done by adding the words 'which means that . . .' So you might say, 'We have 30 refurbished rooms with private bathrooms which means that all your conference delegates will have a comfortable room, a good night's sleep and be fully refreshed for the next day's work.'

If we return to our hotelier, he was visiting a potential conference organizer. In the questions he asked he found out that service and ample car parking were key elements when the sales contact was choosing a hotel. So, before asking for the business, he pointed out that the hotel had a large car park but, to make sure every delegate was looked after, he would keep 12 spaces and put a delegate's name on each place. The hotelier had matched the benefits the potential client wanted with the benefits of staying at his hotel.

The benefits required will be different from one customer to another. The advantage of a personal sales call is that it can be adapted to individual customers' needs to ensure that the benefits you are offering are matched to the benefits the potential customer wants.

## Ask for the order

People do not ask for the order because they fear rejection by the potential customer. However, research has shown that, of 100 salespeople, 90 will not ask for an order and none of them will make a sale. Out of the remaining 10 who ask for an order, nine will be successful. So always ask for the business.

## Close the sale

When you hear the customer say 'How many can you hold in your function room?' or 'Which Saturday nights in July is it free?' you are being given buying signals. The customer is telling you he wants to make a booking, so remember to listen out for the buying signals. When you hear these, ask for the business and confirm the details of the sale.

## Shut up and get out

When you have made the sale, shut up and get out. I say this in the light of bitter experience. I had sold a conference to a customer and as I was about to leave and, perhaps, because I had not established exactly what the prospective customer wanted, I said 'It is a nice, quiet and relaxing location for a conference.' His delegates were looking for something to do in the evenings and I had nothing special to offer them. As a result of my comment I lost the business, so make the sale, shut up and get out.

# Updating the sales database

After you have completed the call you must update the sales database. You need to make a note of what you discussed and the follow-up action that you have agreed. This will then provide a written record of your dealings with each potential customer. You need to know when you should contact them again.

If you have used the example in Figure 12.1 this can be done by attaching a coloured marker to the appropriate month at the top of the form. At the beginning of each month you take out the pages with the tags on for that month. This now provides you with sales information on which you need to take further action.

## Helpful hints to more successful selling

You will make mistakes when you first go out selling. However, I hope that pointing out some of my early mistakes will help you avoid them.

1 Read a book on body language. It will help you to understand the different feelings and emotions that your potential client is going through. It is amazing what different body positions tell us about the person we are talking to.

2 Identify the decision makers. You may have identified a sales contact but he is not really the decision maker because he does not have the power to make a purchasing decision. If you find yourself in this situation ask 'Who would be able to make that decision and would you be able to introduce me to him?'

   Another point to remember is that many decisions are made by secretaries and not their bosses, e.g. where to stay, where to meet for lunch, etc. So always credit the secretary with the possibility that she makes the decisions.

3 Sell a range of products. If we go back to our hotelier selling conferences, he found one client who did not want to use his hotel because he was very happy with his present supplier. However, by asking questions he found out that his sales contact organized the company's Christmas party and had a daughter who was getting married next year. Our hotelier did not sell a conference but he was able to book the two other functions. So, until you have established what is wanted, always be prepared to sell your full range of products, which you identified in the customer/product matrix in Chapter 3. Do not make assumptions.

4 Overcoming complaints. It is very difficult to sell to the customer who has had a bad experience of your business. If this happens in a sales call, immediately stop selling and deal properly with the complaint. Take all the relevant details of the complaint and tell the customer you are going away to investigate it. When you have done this tell them the outcome and invite them back to see how the situation has been rectified. When confidence has been restored you are back in a position to sell.

5 Set personal sales targets. This may be to contact 10 potential customers a month, identify potential revenue of £10,000, or confirm new business of £5,000. Whatever your target, make it realistic. If you then beat your target, set yourself a new and tougher level of achievement.

6 Allocate specific chunks of time for selling. We can all come up with reasons why we have not done any selling this week. So, along with the sales target, allocate a specific amount of time to carry out the sales activity.

7 Encourage your staff to sell. The more people you have selling the greater your sales will be. Do not try and do all the selling yourself. Encourage and motivate others to help you. Your staff are your salesforce; they can identify potential business from both inside and outside your business. If they are successful you can give them an appropriate incentive based on the amount of business they bring in. At worst, you can say thank you for their help.

## Evaluating the results

When you set a clear and quantifiable sales objective at the outset, the evaluation process is much simpler. Your records and sales statistics should provide you with the necessary information for evaluating the results. However, it is worth remembering that when you set the objective you ensure that your systems will collect the necessary information. So, for example, our hotelier would need to separate all the conferences on the full conference delegate pack from the other conference rates, otherwise he could not see if he had reached his objective of 1200 extra rooms.

## Summary

1 You already have some sales ability. You now need to develop the skills and techniques to achieve success.
2 Set a clear and quantifiable overall sales objective at the outset but consider what other objectives you may need to support this.
3 You must always maintain a positive attitude.
4 Create a sales ledger from the information that is available both inside and outside your business.
5 Fill in the gaps in the information by using the telephone.
6 Develop a system for getting appointments that suits you.
7 There are various stages of a personal sales call that you need to understand and practise, e.g. question technique, selling benefits not features, matching benefits, asking for the business, closing the sale.
8 After each sales call update the sales ledger and make a note when to contact the customer again.
9 Ensure that your sales information systems can quantify the objective that you set.

## Key questions

1 How successful is your current sales activity?
2 How can you improve your current attitude?
3 What is your overall sales objective? What are your supporting sales objectives?
4 What are open questions, and what words should you use to ask one?
5 What are the benefits that you can sell to potential customers?
6 How often do you ask for the business?
7 What information systems do you need to set up to make evaluating the sales objective simple?

# 13
## Merchandising

---

## What is it?

Merchandising is about the effort you or others put into maximizing sales and profitability at the point of sale. The two key elements of this are:

1 maximizing,
2 the point of sale.

It is not just a question of increasing the sales but ensuring that you maximize the profit by selling the items with the highest cash profit. For example, if a customer walks into a bar and asks for a gin and tonic, does the bartender know which brand of gin gives the highest cash profit? Does he always serve it when customers do not specify a particular brand, and does he offer a double as well as a single?

The point of sale is the time and place where a customer finally decides to purchase. This could be in the hotel, on the telephone, or outside looking at the menu display. We are fortunate in this industry in that we control all our merchandising points. We are not reliant on third parties putting our products on shelves.

However, our disadvantage is that we have numerous and diverse points of sale.

## Identifying points of sale

Before we can improve our merchandising we need to identify all our points of sale. They can be split into three broad areas:

1 internal,
2 external,
3 incoming.

### Internal

These are the easiest to identify. They include the reception desk, bars, restaurants and the staff. They also include the menu displays in the cabinet outside and the general appearance of the business. So, if menus are dog-eared, dirty plates are not cleared, paint is peeling off, then the appearance of the business will ensure sales are not maximized.

### External

These are away from your business and are third parties who are selling your products and who may be paid a commission for doing so. They include travel agents, conference placement organizers and tourist information centres.

### Incoming

These are enquirers we want to turn into bookings. The enquirer may have seen an advertisement or read about your business but may not finally have decided to make a booking. If a potential customer telephones, do you always convert the enquiry into confirmed business by handling it professionally?

Ask yourself:

1 Do I have a standard for answering the telephone within a specific time-span?

2 Do I record every incoming enquiry by letter or telephone and monitor the conversion rate to a confirmed booking?

3 Is the information logged on the sales database?

I expect the answer is No.

So, the first step is to identify all the points of sale in your business.

## Setting the merchandising objective

The more points of sale there are, the more merchandising objectives you will have. However, they will all fit in with the overall business objectives and support the other promotional tools.

Let us go back to our case studies and look at specific merchandising objectives for each of them.

### The hotel

To convert 50 per cent of all telephone and letter enquiries into confirmed bookings.

### The restaurant

To increase the number of customers that use the restaurant after looking at the menu display outside, from one in 30 to five in 30.

### The pub

To increase the gross profit on liquor from 54 per cent to 56 per cent over the next six months.

### The fast-food restaurant

To increase the number of desserts sold with a main meal from 178 per day to 195 per day.

### *The staff restaurant*

To increase the food gross profit by 5 per cent on the sandwich bar in the next financial year.

We have now set the objectives and analysed where all our points of sale are, but how can we improve our merchandising?

## Improving your merchandising

There are three areas we need to examine in greater detail:

1 analysis of sales points;
2 watch what customers do;
3 reactions to change.

### Analysis of sales points

You should start by identifying all your sales points. Then you need to establish if they are maximizing sales. Ask yourself a number of questions about each one:

1 Does the sales point present well? Is it clean, welcoming and uncluttered, and does it invite the customer to come in and try or buy?
2 Is the information available easily read both day and night. Is the information always available or do staff forget to replenish the brochure racks or change menus?
3 If it is a food area, does it make your eyes light up and your mouth water?
4 Is everything at the right temperature – hot food hot, white wine chilled?
5 Are the staff at the sales point well presented, welcoming, knowledgeable about the products and services available?
6 If the standard is good today, will it be poor tomorrow?
7 How long does the phone ring in reception or other departments before it is answered?
8 How long are customers kept waiting?

The point of this exercise is to enable you to set a minimum standard for every sales point.

Once you have set the standards, you can monitor them so that they are achieved day in and day out.

## Watch what customers do

When was the last time you really watched what happened to customers when they came into your business? Do they come in the front door, ask directions to the restaurant, ignore the bar area, find nobody to welcome them and leave by the side door?

Of course they don't, but how do you know?

You will be amazed at what you can learn by watching customers and their reactions to both staff and the service available. For example:

1 How good are the directional signs? Can people find their way to the toilets or do they have to ask?
2 Identification of maintenance hazards, such as tripping over a worn piece of carpet.
3 Customers' reactions to staff – do they smile back at a member of staff?
4 Customers' attitudes to your business by their comments to their partners, colleagues or guests.
5 Why people buy. What did the member of staff say to encourage them to buy, or how was the item presented?
6 Why people do not buy. Was it out of stock, or did a member of staff not know what it was they were selling?
7 How you can change customers' buying habits. If you present an item in an earthenware pot one day does it sell more or less than if it is plated?
8 How you can increase the frequency of purchase. Did they pick up a brochure and, if so, did they read it or take it with them?
9 How you can increase customers' spend. Were the customers offered a speciality coffee after the meal? Were they offered a large gin and tonic in the bar or just a small one?

From watching customers on a regular basis you will establish how to increase income at the point of sale. This will fall into one of three categories:

1 physical factors such as the menu display or signage;
2 the skills and ability of the staff at the point of sale;
3 customers' reactions to the standard of service you have set.

## Reactions to change

From watching customers you will have identified a number of areas that can be improved or changed. Managing change at the point of sale requires information to be gathered both before and after that change.

So what information might you need?

*Before change*:

1 Analysis of sales mix, e.g. number of dishes served, number of dishes remaining, if sold out when did they sell out?
2 Details of gross profits and costs.
3 Attitudes of customers to the service.
4 The standards that are in operation.
5 How is the information presented to customers?
6 What type of equipment is used?

*After change*:

1 How has the sales mix changed and has it increased sales? If not, why not?
2 Has the profitability increased? Could it be increased still further?
3 What are the customer reactions?
4 What are the new standards that have been introduced and how are they being monitored?
5 How has the presentation of information, food, etc., been improved?

An analysis of the information will show you what has successfully been introduced to increase both sales and profitability. But how could these techniques be used by our case studies?

## *The hotel*

Our hotelier wanted to convert 50 per cent of enquiries into confirmed revenue. This objective was set after he discovered that only 30 per cent of his current enquiries led to business. Telephone enquiries were converted at a rate of 45 per cent but written enquiries at only 15 per cent.

This was particularly worrying because the value of the written enquiry was seven times higher than the telephone enquiry.

The hotel manager established these facts from analysing all enquiries over a two-month period. He then discovered that:

1 By the time a letter had come in, a reply written, typed, signed and sent out, over nine days had elapsed.
2 Some 80 per cent of telephone enquiries came in between 9 a.m. and 12 noon during the week. However, there was only one receptionist on at this time and she could not properly handle all the calls.

So what did he do?

1 He arranged to telephone all incoming letter enquirers on the day the letter was received to discuss the potential customer's particular needs.
2 He employed a telephonist/typist for three hours each weekday morning to deal with incoming calls and ensure the typing was done the same day.
3 A number of standard letters were prepared on the word processor which could easily be adapted for use.
4 He telephoned the potential customer five days later to check that the information had been received and to discuss the booking.

## The restaurant

Over a period of weeks our restaurateur watched what happened when potential customers walked past and stopped to look at the menu display. He discovered that:

1 Only one out of 30 customers actually came in to enquire about booking a meal.
2 Ten out of 30 went to one of the other restaurants nearby and went in.
3 The majority of people walking around looking for a meal was at 7 p.m. when the restaurant was very quiet.

As a result he:

1 Changed the menu display case, illuminated it and made one of the staff responsible for keeping it up to date and well presented.
2 This member of staff had artistic skills and created new displays each week that reflected the different seasons and specialities that were available.
3 A special offer of two meals for the price of one was offered if the meals were ordered before 7.15 p.m.

## The pub

The publican wanted to increase his liquor gross profit from 54 per cent to 56 per cent and in his analysis of sales discovered that:

1 Staff did not know which beers and spirits generated the highest gross profits.
2 All customers could see behind the bar was glasses.
3 The new continental beers were popular but were not always chilled.

He decided to:

1 Train all staff to sell the higher profit items when no particular brand was requested.

2 Negotiate a price reduction on certain lines if sales were increased.
3 Train staff to recommend these lines.
4 Arrange a number of special evenings promoting these lines to create customer awareness.
5 Purchase a number of blackboards which he also used to promote the lines.
6 Buy a small half-barrel which he filled with ice and continental beers and placed on the bar to make it a feature.

## The fast-food restaurant

The manager found that the number of sweets sold with a main course was very low, well under 20 per cent. His market research showed that customers did not know what was available. He took the following action:

1 Introduced a special sweet menu which he placed on all the tables.
2 Created a sweet menu photographic display above the counter.
3 Trained all the staff to offer a sweet to every customer.
4 Gave the staff a badge to wear which said 'Claim a free sweet of your choice if I forget to ask you which one you would like'.
5 Kept staff regularly informed on how many sweets were sold and gave incentives to the person selling the most sweets every week.
6 Revised the target upwards whenever it was beaten.

## The staff restaurant

Each lunchtime the sandwich bar offered 250 sandwiches. The range was 75 cheese and pickle, 25 prawn mayonnaise, 25 chicken tikka, 50 ham and tomato, 25 turkey, 25 egg, and 25 beef and horseradish.

The higher priced and higher profit lines were prawn, chicken and beef. These were always the first items to sell out and this always occurred within 15 minutes of service starting. This reduced the choice and some customers had stopped using the operation. There were usually a few turkey and cheese sandwiches left. The manageress decided to:

1 Increase the number of the popular sandwiches that were prepared and reduce the cheese and turkey.
2 Monitor, on a daily basis, when each type of sandwich sold out.
3 Introduce a higher priced daily special sandwich that was freshly prepared to order.
4 Train the staff to promote this and the higher profit sandwiches.
5 Monitor the gross profit achieved on a weekly basis and inform the staff what they had achieved.

In the examples above we have used a number of merchandising techniques but we have also used sales promotions and PR to show how the different promotional tools can work together.

Our case studies will now monitor the changes they have made in order to check that they achieve the objectives set and, if not, review the action they have taken and revise it.

## Summary

1 Merchandising maximizes profit at the point of sale.
2 Points of sale are internal, external and incoming.
3 The objectives fit into and support the overall business objectives.
4 To improve your merchandising you need to analyse sales, watch what customers do and measure reactions to change.

## Key questions

1 How many sales points are there in your business?
2 What image do they create to potential customers?
3 What are your merchandising objectives?
4 What further information do you need to obtain and how will you collect it?
5 How often do you really watch what happens to your customers?

# 14
# Direct marketing

Direct marketing is one of the fastest growing marketing functions. It is predicted that by the end of the century more money will be spent on direct marketing than on advertising. It has grown up from the days of mail order catalogues, but what is it?

## What is direct marketing?

Direct marketing is all advertising activity that establishes a direct link between your business and existing and potential customers.

Advertising uses a blanket approach. It is seen, heard or read by a large number of people. Direct marketing aims to talk directly to individuals by post, by telephone, in shops, at work or at home. The common factor is that it is precisely targeted to specific people.

So, how could our case studies use this approach?

### The hotel

To create awareness among all past short-break customers about a special painting weekend that is being held in three months' time.

### The restaurant

To make a special introductory offer to conference organizers to sample a meal.

### The fast-food restaurant

To inform potential customers of the home delivery service that is starting in two weeks' time.

### The pub

To send details of this year's Christmas menus to all customers who booked a Christmas party last year.

### The staff restaurant

To tell all heads of department about the new salad bar that is opening.

*To make these into objectives we would need to quantify them, e.g. to sell 20 places on the painting weekend within the next six weeks.*

The main use that you will have for direct marketing is direct mail. It enables you to inform past, current and potential customers about your particular business and any special events and/or offers that are available.

However, if you are storing and using this information on computer, you will need to be aware of the Data Protection Act and the British Code of Advertising Practice.

## The Data Protection Act

If you keep personal information about any customers on computer you will have to register under this Act. In broad terms, this legislation ensures that personal data is:

1 Obtained and processed fairly and lawfully.
2 Used for those purposes described in the Register entry.
3 Adequate, relevant and not excessive.

4 Held no longer than is necessary.
5 Kept securely.

To register (it costs £75 as at February 1992), you should contact:

The Office of the Data Protection Register
Wycliffe House
Water Lane
Wilmslow
Cheshire
SK9 5AF
Tel: (0625) 535777

This office also provides a series of free and very helpful information booklets that will answer your questions.

The holding of personal information by an unregistered user became a criminal offence in May 1986. It is also possible for individuals to seek compensation for any distress caused. Thus your compliance with the Act is vital.

## The Committee of Advertising Practice

This body has a number of information leaflets that cover rules for direct marketing, including list and database management. You can obtain free copies by contacting them at:

Brook House
2–16, Torrington Place
London
WC1E 7HN
Tel: 071 580 5555

You may also find it useful to read the *Consumer's Guide to Direct Marketing* which is available from the Advertising Standards Authority at the same address.

As far as this Code is concerned, direct marketing does not include circulars, leaflets or letters addressed to the householder or occupier. This is because the sender has no knowledge of your personal details.

The rest of this chapter aims to give you a number of helpful hints about creating a mail shot and how to improve its effectiveness.

## Direct mail – helpful hints

1 As for your sales effort and, indeed, combined with it, create an effective database. This is the key to any successful mailing. The information must be up to date and accurate, with names and addresses correctly spelt. The list of names and addresses must be split into the appropriate types of customer, e.g. business traveller, past conference delegates, short-break holidays. This will ensure that you do not waste money by sending an inappropriate letter to a customer, e.g. our hotelier inviting someone who lives 200 miles away to a wedding exhibition.

A great deal of information about customers already exists in your business. There will be reservation or booking details, old function diaries, letters of enquiry, future bookings, compliment letters, etc. If you require a list of potential customers you may need to create a mailing list from local directories and carry out some desk research.

You need to keep updating the information so that new customers are added. However, keep checking that the information is not being duplicated otherwise some customers may receive the same letter twice. This creates a poor image of your business, as well as wasting time and money.

2 Set an objective before writing a word. Clearly establish what you are trying to achieve. Is it creating awareness of your business, making a special offer, or informing

customers about improved services? Ask yourself the following questions:

- Who are you trying to influence?
- What offer are you making, or what service are you selling?
- Why should the potential customer make a purchase or accept the offer?
- When should you write to them?

It is helpful to write down the answers and refer to them as you prepare the letter.

3 Visualize who you are writing to. This is the same technique that we discussed in the chapter on advertising. It is much easier to write to someone if you have a mental picture of them.

4 Sell benefits. Remember, it is not what it is, it is what it does. What benefits are the potential customers looking for? People buy for one of these reasons: to help their families, feel secure, impress others, make money, save money, save time and effort, gain pleasure, improve themselves, belong to a group. So, appeal to one of these buying motives.

5 Differentiate yourself from your competitors. Always look at the extra benefits that you have to offer and that are different from the ones offered by the competitors, e.g. a special welcome for children.

6 If you cannot make a special offer, then can you say something of interest? For example, the opening of a newly refurbished bar, or the holding of prices for another six months.

7 Use testimonials. Third-party endorsements from respected and satisfied customers are very powerful. They can be used as a headline or in the body of the letter,

provided you have prior consent of the person concerned.

8 Be accurate. Never make claims that are difficult to support.

9 Use a headline at the top of the letter. The purpose of this is to gain the reader's attention and encourage them to find out what else is in the letter. It can be typed in capitals, bold or underlined to increase its impact.

10 Never send out Dear Sir/Madam letters. Every letter must be personalised. This can easily be achieved with most word-processing packages, but remember, if you do use a computer, you are reminded about the Data Protection Act and the codes of practice.

11 Double-check all spellings. If you are using a word-processor then you probably have a spell-check system. If you don't then ask someone else to check the letter.

12 Never 'pp' a letter for someone else. If the person whose name is on the bottom of the letter is unavailable then sign their name for them. The likelihood of anyone knowing it was not signed by Fred Bloggs is very remote and it avoids the implication of not being bothered to sign the letter.

13 If you want to emphasize a particular point, use bold type or underlining. Avoid changing the typeface, such as introducing italics. Another way is to use a 'PS' at the end of the letter.

14 There is no right or wrong length for a letter. The important fact is that it maintains the reader's interest and encourages them to read to the end. Obviously, the longer the letter the more difficult this is to achieve.

15 Give the letter 'you' appeal. Keep the use of 'I' and 'we' to a minimum and maximize 'you' and 'your'. For example: 'We provide' will become 'you will receive'.

16  Be careful how the letter is put into the envelope. Make sure it is neatly folded and signed, with the letter heading visible as you open the envelope.

17  People like to receive letters, and some people look forward to opening the post. If someone asks for a brochure, then send them a letter as well. It will reinforce your message and increase the chance of making a sale.

18  The margin on the left-hand side of the letter should be one inch wide because it makes it easier to read.

19  Set the typeface so that it prints no more than 60 characters to a line. This also makes it easier to read.

20  Check the length of sentences. The opening sentence should not be more than 14 words and other sentences should not have more than 24. The more words, the less likelihood of it being read.

21  Do not use jargon or pompous language. Keep it simple, using everyday language.

22  Do not use three words when one will do.

23  If you expect a reply from a customer then either enclose a stamped addressed envelope or a reply-paid envelope.

24  We referred to the AIDA principle in the chapter on advertising. It can be a useful check on a direct mail letter. Ask yourself if your letter gains Attention, Interest, Desire, Action.

These points will help you to improve the success rate of your direct mail letters. However, if you still find it difficult you could ask a copywriter – it is not as expensive as you might think.

The great advantage of direct mail is that it is sent to specific people who have used, or might use, your business. At first glance, it might look expensive with stationery, postage and labour. However, because it is specifically targeted, it can be very cost effective.

You must monitor each mail shot to assess its effectiveness. This can be done by asking respondents to quote a special reference when they telephone or to complete a particular form and send it back. Try different methods when you start so that you can establish which are the most successful for your business.

## Summary

1 Direct marketing is a form of advertising which communicates directly with individual potential customers.
2 It comes in a variety of forms but you are most likely to use direct mail.
3 There are many ways by which you can increase the success rate of direct mail, but the key is the AIDA principle.
4 Monitor each mail shot to identify success and failure.
5 Direct mail is better targeted than other promotional tools so it can be very cost effective.

## Key questions

1 How often have you used direct mail, and what success have you achieved?
2 What information do you have on past customers and how accessible is it?
3 How can you create a database of potential customers?
4 How will you monitor the success of your next mail shot?
5 What offer will you be making in that letter?

# 15
# Marketing and promotional calendars

We have already highlighted the need to create action plans in Chapter 6, because your plan needs to be properly managed. In that chapter we talked about using action plans for introducing new products or product changes. However, the same discipline should be applied to all aspects of your marketing. The process will help you to:

1 Clarify exactly what has to be done and by when.
2 Create ownership of the plan with everyone involved.
3 Change and update the plan as and when required.

However, in even a small hospitality business you may have 20 or 30 individual marketing action plans that detail everything from market research to promotional activities. To make the management of this process easier you will find it useful to create:

1 The marketing calendar.
2 The promotional calendar.

(see Figures 15.1 and 15.2).

These will enable you to:

1 Ensure that there are no clashes of activity in any particular month, such as carrying out market research in the same business community for two separate services.

2  Monitor what needs to be happening each month.
3  Ensure that deadlines for printing, advertising, mailing, etc. are all met.

The easiest way of illustrating how this works is to use the example of our hotelier. Let us take three marketing activities that have been identified in earlier chapters. The action plans for each are illustrated in Tables 15.1, 15.2 and 15.3, and are as follows:

- *Action Plan 1*. Objective: to increase the number of wedding receptions with over 100 guests from 26 to 32 in the next financial year.

- *Action Plan 2*. Objective: to sell an extra 1200 conference bed nights in the next financial year at an all inclusive rate of £75.00.

- *Action Plan 3*: Objective: to convert 50 per cent of all telephone and letter enquiries into confirmed bookings.

In the action plans, the marketing calendar and the promotional calendar we have identified how the hotelier put his plan together. You will realize that this is just a small section of his overall plan, however it does highlight a number of learning points.

If this were your plan, what would you do to improve it? Before reading on, look at the plans and decide:

1  what alterations you might make;
2  what are the good points about the plans.

**Table 15.1** The marketing objective: to increase the number of wedding receptions with over 100 guests sold next year from 26 to 32

| What has to be done? | How? | By whom? | By when? | Review |
|---|---|---|---|---|
| Carry out research into customer needs | Write to all past wedding organizers to establish their attitudes to the hotel | Hotel manager | 1 May | |
| | Interview 20 couples who are getting married to identify their requirements | Hotel manager | 1 May | |
| | Talk to 50 customers who have attended a wedding in the hotel in the last 12 months | Deputy and asst manager | 1 May | |
| Devise new promotional material | Create new menus | Head chef | 1 July | |
| | Brief printer for new artwork and copy | Hotel manager | 1 July | |
| | Proof-read all material and send to printer | Hotel manager | 1 August | |
| | Print material to be ready | Printer | 1 September | |

**Table 15.1** Continued

| What has to be done? | How? | By whom? | By when? | Review |
|---|---|---|---|---|
| Organize a wedding exhibition | Send out invitations to exhibitors | Hotel manager | 1 May | |
| | Agree final list of exhibitors | Hotel manager | 21 July | |
| | Agree final details of the wedding exhibition | Hotel manager | 1 August | |
| | Send out invitations to exhibition | Hotel manager | 1 September | |
| Create awareness of exhibition and new wedding package | Put up a promotional table in reception area | Deputy manager | 10 September | |
| | Create a wedding display in exterior showcases | Housekeeper | 1 September | |
| | Brief advertising agency to create adverts | Hotel manager | 1 August | |
| | Agree final advertising copy | Hotel manager | 1 September | |
| | Advertising campaign starts | Advertising agency | 21 September | |
| | Send out press release to local paper about exhibition | Hotel manager | 10 October | |
| | Organize special offer of free night's accommodation for anyone making a definite booking at the exhibition | Hotel manager | 10 October | |

| Hold wedding exhibition on 17 November and follow up action | Take names and addresses of everyone attending | Head receptionist | 17 November |
| | Take photographs of event and send out with press release after event | Hotel manager | 19 November |
| | Direct mail to everyone that attended the event | Hotel manager | 20 November |
| Evaluation of event | Review success and failure of the event | The management team | 31 November |
| | Agree the plan of action for next year | Hotel manager | 7 December |
| | Identify the number of bookings made and compare with target | Hotel manager | 1 January onwards |
| | Use staff noticeboard to keep staff informed about bookings | Asst manager | 1 January onwards |

**Table 15.2** The marketing objective: to sell an extra 1200 conference bed nights in the next financial year at the all-inclusive rate of £75

| What has to be done? | How? | By whom? | By when? | Review |
|---|---|---|---|---|
| Review the competition | Identify the main competitors in a 40-mile radius | Head receptionist | 1 July | |
| | Carry out telephone research to establish the conference packages that they offer | Head receptionist | 1 August | |
| | Analyse the standards of the competition | Deputy manager | 1 August | |
| Establish the size and needs of the market | Identify the 150 top companies within a 40-mile radius | Manager's secretary | 1 September | |
| | Direct mail market research to personnel and sales directors within these companies | Hotel manager | 1 October | |
| | Follow up telephone calls to fill in information gaps | Secretary | 1 November | |
| | Create a sales database from the above information | Hotel manager | 1 December | |

| Revise the conference package | Change the package in the light of the research | Hotel manager | 1 September |
| | Reprint the promotional material | Hotel manager | 1 November |
| Create awareness | Develop a sales presenter for use in sales calls | Manager's secretary | 1 October |
| | Carry out 10 sales calls per month to top 150 companies | Hotel manager | Ongoing 1 December |
| | Advertise in local Chamber of Trade directory | Hotel manager | 1 January |

**Table 15.3**   The marketing objective: to convert 50 per cent of all telephone and letter enquiries into confirmed bookings

| What has to be done? | How? | By whom? | By when? | Review |
|---|---|---|---|---|
| Review current practice | Carry out desk research to establish current conversion level | Manager's secretary | 1 May | |
| | Establish the weaknesses in the booking system by making mystery calls and sending enquiry letter from a friend | Hotel manager | 1 June | |
| | Write down all the weaknesses in the current system | Deputy manager | 1 July | |
| Set new standards | Agree and write down all the new standards | Deputy manager | 1 September | |
| | Train all relevant staff in new standards | Deputy manager | 1 October | |
| | Create a series of standard letters on the word processor | Hotel manager | 1 September | |
| | Employ a telephonist to help in reception in the morning | Asst manager | 1 September | |

| Monitor standards | Set up a system to monitor all incoming enquiries | Asst manager | 1 September |
| | Record all business that is not converted to a confirmed sale | Head receptionist | Ongoing from 1 October |
| | Personal telephone call to enquirers to answer any questions and ask for the business | Hotel manager | Ongoing from 1 October |

| Area | April | May | June | July | August | September | October | November | December |
|---|---|---|---|---|---|---|---|---|---|
| Increase wedding bookings | Research among past users, young couples and past guests<br>Send out suppliers' invitations to exhibition | | Create new menus<br>Brief printer | Finalize print copy<br>Finalize wedding exhibition<br>Brief advertising agency | Print to be ready<br>Send out invitations to exhibition<br>Wedding display in outside showcase<br>Agree advertising copy | Set up promotional table<br>Advertising starts | Send out press release<br>Organize sales promotion for free accommodation | Hold wedding exhibition<br>Send out press release after the event<br>Direct mail to everyone that attended<br>Review the event | Agree plan of action for next year<br>Set up information on staff noticeboard to keep them informed<br>Regularly update |
| Develop conference market | | | Identify the competition | Carry out telephone research<br>Analyze the competition | Identify the top 150 companies<br>Change the package in the light of research | Direct mail research to top 150 companies<br>Develop a sales presenter | Telephone research to 150 companies to fill in gaps<br>Reprint promotional material | Create a sales database | Start 10 sales calls per month<br>Organize advert in local Chamber of Trade publication |

| Area | April | May | June | July | August | September | October | November | December |
|------|-------|-----|------|------|--------|-----------|---------|----------|----------|
| Improve enquiry conversion rate | Carry out desk research | Establish current weaknesses in the system with mystery calls | Compile list of weaknesses | | Agree and write down all new standards<br><br>Create a series of standard letters on the word processor<br><br>Employ telephonist<br><br>Set up monitoring system | Train all the staff | Record all business that is not converted to a sale<br><br>Start telephone policy by hotel manager | | |

**Figure 15.1** The marketing calendar

*April*

Direct mail to exhibition suppliers

*May*

None

*June*

Brief for printer

*July*

Finalize print copy
Brief advertising agency

*August*

Direct mail invitations to exhibition
Wedding display in outside showcase
Finalize advertising copy
Create new direct mail letters

*September*

Set up wedding promotional table
Advertising campaign starts
Direct mail to top 150 companies sent out
Sales presenter is produced

*October*
Send out press release
Organize wedding sales promotion
Reprint conference material

*November*
Wedding exhibition takes place
Press release to be sent out
Direct mail to attendees at exhibition
Create a sales database

*December*
Set up PR activity on staff noticeboard
Start personal sales calls
Organize advert in Local Chamber of Trade publications

**Figure 15.2** The promotional calendar

Your comments may have included some of the following:

1 There is very little happening in May and perhaps the action dates could be revised.
2 The plan incorporates a good variety of promotional tools and involves a wide range of people within the hotel.
3 The PR activity is not sustained; it is rather sporadic.
4 There is a lot of research to undertake in April, would this be realistic?
5 Is it also realistic to agree the next year's plan of action in December for weddings before we have evaluated the results?
6 Should we be revising the conference package in August and planning to reprint it when research is still ongoing in September/October?
7 Is the idea of the hotel manager starting a series of personal calls in December acceptable when so much is happening with Christmas parties?
8 Could the enquiry programme be better organized by bringing more action into July, or was it that the hotel manager knew he would be on holiday?

The purpose of the exercise is to provide a simple framework that you can look at and make changes to.

Our hotelier would consider the above and then return to the plan and fine-tune it. He would address each point and alter the dates and activity accordingly. In this way he can ensure that it will fit comfortably into his overall business plan.

This point is further illustrated in Figure 17.1 which shows the index to a business plan and identifies where these sections would fit in.

# 16
## The distribution network

The distribution network covers the ways in which goods and services reach the customer. However, there is a big difference between manufacturing and service industries.

In manufacturing it will involve:

1 All aspects of the transport fleet.
2 Stocks in the warehouse or regional depots.
3 The management and organization of the salesforce.
4 The after-sales support.
5 The level of production in the factory.

Many of these items rely on heavy plant, storage areas and materials, e.g. delivery vans and spare parts.

In a service industry we do not have a transport fleet, a factory, regional depots or a salesforce – or do we?

Your transport fleet is all your management and staff who take orders from customers, process them, serve and then make a charge. These same people decide how much stock is in the food and liquor store and how much needs to be produced, and they are trying to obtain more business.

In other words, in a service industry the main emphasis of the distribution network is your staff.

## What are the key areas of distribution for your business?
### The minor influences

These are the physical factors that influence the level of delivery to customers. They include:

1 The location of your business.
2 The design and layout of the building.
3 The standard of décor.
4 The style and quality of fixtures and fittings.
5 The size of facilities, e.g. 60-seater restaurant.
6 The availability of car parking.
7 The location of individual facilities within your business, e.g. how close is the kitchen to your largest function room?

These factors can be changed but such changes will often require capital investment.

## The major influences

Staff attitudes in your hospitality business have been constantly referred to throughout this book. Let me remind you of just a few:

1 Being customer-oriented so that the customer comes first and is always well looked after; not just on one visit, but the next one and the one after that.
2 Asking questions to find out what customers want, and feeding the information back to you, the manager.
3 Selling other services or extra items to existing customers.
4 A source of good ideas.
5 Wanting to be kept informed about what is happening in the business.

Staff should be viewed as one of your most important assets in the same way as the building, stock levels, etc. I am not suggesting that you become submissive to their every request. However, they need to be kept informed and involved in your marketing activity because they will be better motivated, give better service and bring in more business.

Another way of looking at it is to liken the situation to external and internal marketing. Most of this book has been involved with external marketing because it is activity that will influence customers, create awareness and complete a sale. Internal marketing is about what goes on with your staff inside your business. So how can you improve and develop your internal markets?

## The role of training

Some time ago I worked for a regional director who had a particular saying that puts training into perspective. He said:

Training sets good standards
Good standards bring in more sales
More sales increase profit
Increased profit keeps you and me in a job.

Training is a starting point because it enables all staff to achieve your standards of service. Good standards not only have to be set but they must be achieved consistently, irrespective of who provides the service or cooks the meal.

Unfortunately, when sales decline, such as in a recession, one of the first areas to be cut is training. This is usually followed by a reduction of the marketing expenditure.

This may be understandable, but to my mind is short sighted and very damaging to the business. Let me explain. If the overall market for your hospitality products and services is in decline, then the only way to increase or maintain sales is to take business away from competitors. To achieve this you need better standards and the budget to promote your business to potential customers, thus the need for maintaining training and marketing.

There is one other positive reason for concentrating on marketing during a decline in the market. It enables you to focus your activity on precise business objectives and will mean that you will come out of the decline stronger and fitter than your competitors.

## How can you get the best out of staff?

We have already described staff as an asset. When you consider the costs of recruitment, replacement and training they may be seen as a very valuable asset indeed.

So how can we retain staff and get the best out of them? These are a few examples:

1 *Provide knowledge of results*. Staff work much better when they know what is happening. They are genuinely interested and can be far more helpful when they understand the difficulties facing the business. However, you must give them information regularly and in a form they can understand.

In the chapter on PR we referred to the use of staff noticeboards. These can be used very effectively to communicate information, provided that such information is clear and updated on a regular basis.

Imagine you have spent time creating and explaining a graph that shows sales this year against last year. If you keep it accurate for six weeks and then stop, consider what message you are sending to your staff – 'I have stopped being concerned or interested and I do not need any more business.'

Always give information that can be understood. How many staff understand terms like 'gross profits against net profits', or 'food cost percentages'?

So make the information simple. Consider presenting information graphically rather than just using figures.

2 *Encourage staff input*. You and your management team alone do not have all the good ideas. The more people you have helping you the better. So encourage ideas, and when staff bring them in to you do not dismiss them out of hand. Show a genuine interest and suggest discussing the idea with others. If you stifle ideas from staff they will stop putting them forward, and you never know how good the next idea is going to be.

3 *Say 'thank you'*. Every one of us likes to be told that we are doing a good job; we feel better and usually try even harder afterwards. The words 'thank you' and 'well done' cost nothing but are rarely used enough. They show staff that:
(a) you noticed;
(b) you appreciated what they have done.

4 *Watch your own attitude*. We have already talked about being positive and remaining positive. This is just a reminder to maintain that attitude at all times and leave domestic problems at home. How often does a manager leave home under a cloud and then bring that cloud to work? The result is that the cloud bursts and deposits its contents on the staff, leaving them wet and uncomfortable.

5 *Talk to staff*. This may be obvious but staff are regularly ignored or taken for granted. So make a point of showing an interest in what they are doing.

6 *Consider incentives*. I do not believe that everyone should be on an incentive scheme all the time. Such schemes become the norm and may cease to have any impact. But incentives can work if they are for specific time-spans and for achieving specific targets.

7 *Use appraisals*. Too often appraisals are seen as a negative experience, a chance to tell people how bad they are. Appraisals are a useful management tool that can help, guide, motivate and reward your key staff. So learn how to carry out positive appraisals and then hold them on a regular basis.

Be very careful about using fear as a motivator because it can only have a short-term, shock effect. If used regularly it is threatening and unproductive and leads to high labour turnover. You need to set targets and objectives but it is not 'if you do not achieve them, then dire consequences will follow'.

Your staff are the key to your success, so never forget that. It is not a question of you being managed by your staff but of involving them so that the objectives set are achieved.

## Summary

1 Distribution in a manufacturing industry is more concerned with physical factors.
2 Physical factors do influence the distribution network in the hospitality industry but the key factor is your staff.
3 Consider the difference between external and internal marketing.
4 The process starts with training, which achieves consistent standards which leads to more business.
5 There are many ways of getting the best out of your staff. Look at ways to achieve this.

## Key questions

1 What physical factors influence your distribution network? Can they be altered or changed?
2 How involved are your staff with the business?
3 How can this involvement be improved?
4 What emphasis do you put on training?
5 How can your training programmes be developed?
6 What ideas are you going to adopt to involve your staff more and get the best out of them?

# 17
## Pulling it all together: the business plan

Whatever type of establishment you may manage or help to manage, always remember it is a business that has to make a profit. However good the marketing, efforts will not add up to much if you do not make the most of resources, control costs and plan investments prudently.

You need a vehicle to pull all the strands together. You need a business plan.

### The definition of a business plan

A business plan is a statement of the actions and resources required by a business to sustain and grow its activities.

But why prepare a business plan? Why prepare yet another document which may seem to overlay all the other plans and decisions you now know must be addressed? Why do it, when time is at a premium and moving on too fast to be caught meaningfully in a collection of pages more relevant, it may seem, to a multi-national than the day-to-day, customer-oriented service industry of which you are a member?

The answer, once you hack it, will be only too obvious.

The act of preparing a business plan is a discipline in itself: it not only helps you co-ordinate all the efforts which are directed towards achievement but provides a framework within which you may think through, and challenge, individual decisions and action plans.

Above all, it provides a financial framework which you may use to summarize income, expenditure and cash flow and validate the 'bottom line'.

The business plan is a management tool that targets achievement and sets out the costs of all the resources needed to achieve those targets. The plan, however, is sterile if it is not informed by a marketing-oriented approach – all the activities this book has discussed.

Further, it must be a 'live' document that is capable of being up-dated to show *actual* performance against *forecast* performance so that key variances may be identified and corrective action taken.

Remember, too, that the business plan is a powerful means of communication and that its contents may be modified to suit its various purposes.

For instance, you may use the plan to help raise capital or to negotiate an overdraft.

For this purpose the plan needs to contain the information that will help the decision-maker come to an informed decision about a loan, as well as the financial projections that demonstrate the profit – the bottom line – which may be achieved with the help of additional investment or working capital.

You may wish to use the plan as a means of communicating to all the staff your ambitions for the year ahead so that they may identify how their own contributions relate to the overall scheme.

For this purpose, clearly, you omit financial or other information which you would wish to remain confidential or which you may assess to be too sensitive for general release. You would not, for instance, wish to broadcast those elements of your strategy that might be of interest to the competition.

You may also wish to display action plans, like the marketing and promotional plans, so that your team is continually reminded of what is being achieved and what still needs to be done, by whom and by when.

The plan contains the key targets that must be achieved if the business is to survive and thrive. The targets may be expressed in profit terms, or by turnover or by units (number of covers, occupancy rates, sales units, etc.) and it would be sensible to provide each profit centre (chef, reception, bar, health club, coffee shop, wines, etc.) or each cost centre (housekeeper, maintenance, office, etc.) with their own targets

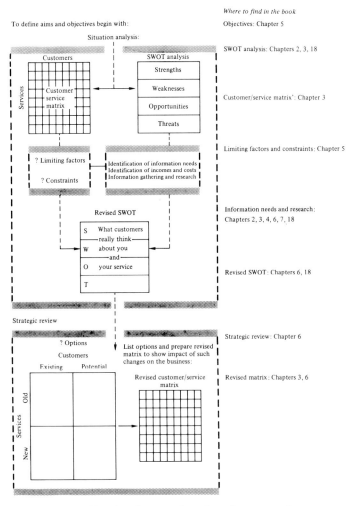

**Figure 17.1** The business planning framework

shown month by month so that they can see how their performance measures up. You will expect them to decide what remedial action they should take if they are not achieving their forecasts (to which of course they will have contributed) and be able to discuss with you what and why aspects of their job may be going wrong.

However the plan is used it must be seen to hang together: it must be coherent and it must be based on the best information you can gather to ensure that it addresses the realities of your marketplace and aims to exploit genuine opportunities.

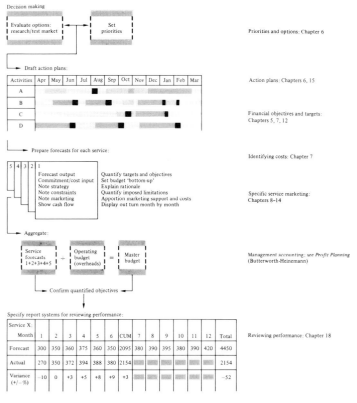

**Figure 17.1** Continued

Thus the marketing input is vital and is the reason why the plan will be driven by all the aspects of the development of your marketing strategy.

It will detail the analysis of the situation the business is in, the information you have gathered to determine its new direction and its strengths and weaknesses, its opportunities and threats.

The business plan summarizes the strategic review that you have made and contains the lists of priorities for the future.

It details the key objective for each facet of the business and elaborates how the marketing mix of advertising, selling and PR are to be employed to help achieve these objectives.

It expresses, in financial terms, the receipts for each part of the business, the direct costs (variable and fixed) that must be borne as part and parcel of the delivery of these services, and the overheads which result from the management, operations and marketing of the services.

Specifically, it will contain plans for the development of key services and utilisation of resources without which you now know the business will flounder and fail to develop.

These significant plans will be prepared with their own financial forecasts and cashflows.

In summary, the business plan is a synopsis of all the major management decisions which have been made and which are yet to be made to ensure a future, managed direction and the survival and prosperity of the business in a highly competitive environment.

Market-driven business planning may be summarised through the application of the *framework* schematic (Figure 17.1): There are four key stages:

1  situation analysis,
2  strategic review,
3  decision making,
4  monitoring and review.

By now none of these stages should appear daunting: this book has helped you to explore what each stage may involve so the *framework* should be seen as an additional overall guide to the process, a map to keep you on course and to help you avoid missing out on the logic.

## What a business plan looks like

The format of a business plan may vary, but Figure 17.2 shows just one way in which it may be composed. This comprehensive format is especially valid for your first edition: as the process is repeated you may be able to pay less attention to the 'background' and concentrate more on the detail and sophistication of the individual plans.

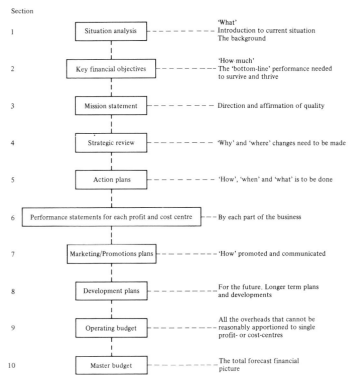

Section

1  Situation analysis — — — — — — — — 'What'
   Introduction to current situation
   The background

2  Key financial objectives — — — — — — — 'How much'
   The 'bottom-line' performance needed
   to survive and thrive

3  Mission statement — — — — — — — — Direction and affirmation of quality

4  Strategic review — — — — — — — — 'Why' and 'where' changes need to be made

5  Action plans — — — — — — — — 'How', 'when' and 'what' is to be done

6  Performance statements for each profit and cost centre — — — By each part of the business

7  Marketing/Promotions plans — — — — — — — 'How' promoted and communicated

8  Development plans — — — — — — — For the future. Longer term plans and developments

9  Operating budget — — — — — — — All the overheads that cannot be reasonably apportioned to single profit- or cost-centres

10 Master budget — — — — — — — The total forecast financial picture

**Figure 17.2**

## Summary

This book is about marketing. Marketing drives the business and dictates the business plan. To appreciate the value of pulling all the threads together in one overall summary – the business plan – review, if you wish, the preceding chapters.

Consider, as you do so, what actions you may wish to implement, when these actions will be undertaken and what is their cost. Follow the examples of our case study companies and see how you may decide to follow through our suggestions and apply them to your own business.

*Chapter 2*:
Find out what customers think.
*Chapter 3*:
What are the strengths of the business?
*Chapter 4*:
What research do you need to undertake?
*Chapter 5*:
What should be the priorities and objectives?
*Chapter 6*:
What do you need to improve and what will it cost?
*Chapter 7*:
What is the balance between income and price?
*Chapter 8–14*:
How are you to market and what is the cost?
*Chapter 16*:
Do the staff share the vision, and what training is required?

## Key questions

1 Can you manage without a business plan?
2 How can you involve the staff in the preparation of the plan?
3 To what purposes may the plan be put?
4 How can you ensure that the plans hang together?
5 What will be the most efficient and effective way of monitoring performance and comparing *actual* with *forecast*?

# 18
# The re-analysis of your business

You have now reached the last chapter. You will have a far greater understanding of marketing and how it can improve the profitability of your business. However, the profit must be sustainable. It is not a question of making a quick buck today and forgetting about tomorrow.

Sustainable profit is based on the business that you have gained from new customers and from existing customers buying more frequently. Thus the business grows and moves forward.

## Marketing is like a bicycle wheel

We have already likened marketing to a bicycle wheel. The marketing process is like a bicycle journey. At the start you set business objectives. These are where you want the business to go. In other words, they are your destination.

We then need to get on our marketing bicycle, put pressure on the pedals and move through the marketing cycle. Each time we move through one revolution, we are nearer the destination. How far we have moved will depend on other outside factors, such as the state of the economy. So the journey could be described as uphill or down, depending on whether the economy is strong or weak.

The important factor to remember is that marketing is an ongoing process. It does not stop after just one revolution; it moves forward again over new ground towards its objectives. The second revolution will be different from the first because the market situation will have changed. Some of the marketing activities you have undertaken will have succeeded, others may need to be looked at again and developed or improved.

If we continue to use the bicycle analogy, then you may have to change gears. That is increase or decrease the spend on the promotional tools. It could be that the objectives need to be re-defined and that the final destination of your journey will be slightly different.

As you complete the marketing cycle you need to re-analyse your business.

## The re-analysis of your business

At the start of the marketing process we asked a number of questions to identify where we were starting from.

We now need to ask similar questions to establish how far we have gone, so that we can consider what action now needs to be taken.

Ask yourself:

1 What are your current and potential customers' attitudes towards your business?
2 Who are your current customers and what services are they buying?
3 How have these changed from your original customer/service matrix?
4 How much are the various customers spending per visit and how often do they come?
5 Has this declined or increased?
6 What are the reasons for the change?
7 How much have sales and profits been increased? Did they meet the objective set?
8 How successful have each of the promotional tools been?
9 How have customers heard about your business?

10 What has the competition been doing?
11 What are the current strengths, weaknesses, opportunities and threats of the business?

## Carry out another SWOT analysis

In Chapter 3 we looked at a SWOT analysis for our fast-food restaurant. This helped us analyse the business in a structured way. It is also a key tool in the re-analysis process because it will identify how your business has changed and what areas you now need to concentrate on. You should compare how the following SWOT has changed from the first one our fast-food manager produced.

### Fast-food restaurant SWOT analysis

*Strengths*:

● Good high-street location.
● Excellent local reputation.
● Manager is experienced and well known and has agreed to stay.
● Home delivery service has been a great success.
● The evening shift has attracted a number of women returners to work.
● The manager has set up an anti-litter campaign with the local Chamber of Trade, which has created considerable goodwill.
● Some new kitchen equipment has been purchased to increase the speed of service.
● Lunchtime business between 2.15 p.m. and 2.45 p.m. has increased by 23 per cent.
● The menu has successfully been extended to incorporate jacket potatoes and fillings, which now accounts for 15 per cent of sales.

*Weaknesses*:

- More delivery equipment is needed to cope with the evening delivery service.
- Lunchtime shortage of staff has caused a rise in customer complaints of 17 per cent.
- Local pressure group has switched attention to the quantity and type of packaging used.
- Decline in the quality of staff available for employment at lunchtime.
- Décor is looking drab.
- Lunch sales have fallen by 8 per cent on Friday and 9 per cent on Monday.
- Average spend has only risen by 2 per cent against an inflation factor of 5 per cent.

*Opportunities*:

- To purchase more equipment to expand the evening delivery service.
- To create a series of sales promotions to reverse the trends on Monday and Friday lunchtime and increase the sales between 2.15 p.m. and 2.45 p.m. by a further 10 per cent.
- To combine sales promotion with re-training of all staff.
- To see if any women returners are interested in working school term lunchtimes only.
- To start a recycling scheme to support local hospital scanner appeal to be launched at the time of the competitor opening.
- To provide a staff incentive to increase the average spend per customer by 47p.
- To refurbish décor of restaurant area.

*Threats*:

- New fast-food outlet to be opened in two months' time.
- Total labour market has declined by 2 per cent.
- Proposal by the local council to pedestrianize certain areas

of the town and reduce the times that vans can deliver goods.
● A predicted rise in inflation of 4.5 per cent over the next 12 months.

This SWOT analysis has seen some strengths remain, new weaknesses emerge, and the creation of new opportunities.

However it has also identified some new information requirements. You will remember that the information requirements will fall into three areas:

1 product,
2 customers,
3 competition.

Our fast-food manager will need to find out:

1 Attitudes towards the current décor and establish how it should be improved.
2 Why so many more customers are complaining.
3 What the new competition intends to offer and how it will promote itself.

Thus the marketing cycle has completed one revolution and the manager will now start the planning process for the next revolution, and so on.

While a business remains marketing oriented it has the best opportunity to grow and sustain that growth. But marketing never stands still, it is a management process that must change, develop and anticipate.

At the start of this book we described marketing as a simple process. It is simple because it is logical, provided you always remember to look at all problems through the eyes of your customers. You will achieve success if you always maintain that approach, set clear objectives and plan ahead.

There is one final question.

When are you going to adopt the principles and ideas that have been put forward in this book? You have invested time and money getting this far. Do not just put the book down.

Make a decision now to adopt and implement a marketing philosophy throughout your business. You, your staff and your business will all benefit.

## Summary

1 The marketing process is like a bicycle journey.
2 The marketing cycle is like a bicycle wheel. It does not go over the same ground each time as it is moving you closer to your business objectives.
3 Your business will move forward so you need to carry out a regular re-analysis and ask yourself a number of key questions.
4 When you reach this stage carry out another SWOT analysis.
5 Identify further information needs and start the process again.
6 Marketing is simple because it is logical.
7 Always remember to approach difficulties through the eyes of customers.

## Key questions

1 How much of your profit is sustainable?
2 How often do you look at business problems through the eyes of customers?
3 When are you going to start the marketing process for your business?
4 Who are you going to involve in the process?
5 What benefits are you planning to achieve?

# Index